Access to History

General Editor: Keith Randell

France in Revolution

Duncan Townson

Hodder & Stoughton

A MEMBER OF THE HODDER HEADLINE GROUP

The cover illustration shows *La Liberté* by Nanine Vallain (courtesy La Musée de la Revolution Française, Vizille).

Some other titles in the series:

Russia, Poland and the Ottoman Empire **1725–1800** Andrina Stiles	ISBN 0 340 53334 X
Europe and the Enlightened Despots Walter Oppenheim	ISBN 0 340 53559 8
The Unification of Germany, 1815–90 Andrina Stiles	ISBN 0 340 51810 3
The Unification of Italy, 1815–90 Andrina Stiles	ISBN 0 340 51809 X
Russia 1815–81 Russell Sherman	ISBN 0 340 54789 8
The Concert of Europe: International Relations **1815–70** John Lowe	ISBN 0 340 53496 6
France 1814–70: Monarchy, Republic and Empire Keith Randell	ISBN 0 340 51805 7
France: The Third Republic 1870–1914 Keith Randell	ISBN 0 340 55569 6

British Library Cataloguing in Publication Data

Townson, W. D. (William Duncan), *1927–*
France in revolution.–(Access to History).
1. France, history
I. Title   II. Series
944.04

ISBN 0 340 53494 X

First published 1990
Impression number 10   9   8   7   6
Year   1998   1997   1996   1995

Typeset by Wearset, Boldon, Tyne & Wear
Printed in Great Britain for Hodder and Stoughton Educational, a division of Hodder Headline Plc, 338 Euston Road, London NW1 3BH
by Page Bros, Norwich

Contents

Preface

To the general reader

Although the *Access to History* series has been designed with the needs of students studying the subject at higher examination levels very much in mind, it also has a great deal to offer the general reader. The main body of the text (i.e. ignoring the Study Guides at the ends of chapters) forms a readable and yet stimulating survey of a coherent topic as studied by historians. However, each author's aim has not merely been to provide a clear explanation of what happened in the past (to interest and inform): it has also been assumed that most readers wish to be stimulated into thinking further about the topic and to form opinions of their own about the significance of the events that are described and discussed (to be challenged). Thus, although no prior knowledge of the topic is expected on the reader's part, she or he is treated as an intelligent and thinking person throughout. The author tends to share ideas and possibilities with the reader, rather than passing on numbers of so-called 'historical truths'.

To the student reader

There are many ways in which the series can be used by students studying History at a higher level. It will, therefore, be worthwhile thinking about your own study strategy before you start your work on this book. Obviously, your strategy will vary depending on the aim you have in mind, and the time for study that is available to you.

If, for example, you want to acquire a general overview of the topic in the shortest possible time, the following approach will probably be the most effective:

1 Read Chapter 1 and think about its contents.
2 Read the 'Making notes' section at the end of Chapter 2 and decide whether it is necessary for you to read this chapter.
3 If it is, read the chapter, stopping at each heading or * to note down the main points that have been made.
4 Repeat stage 2 (and stage 3 where appropriate) for all the other chapters.

If, however, your aim is to gain a thorough grasp of the topic, taking however much time is necessary to do so, you may benefit from carrying out the same procedure with each chapter, as follows:

1 Read the chapter as fast as you can, and preferably at one sitting.
2 Study the flow diagram at the end of the chapter, ensuring that you understand the general 'shape' of what you have just read.

3   Read the 'Making notes' section (and the 'Answering essay questions' section, if there is one) and decide what further work you need to do on the chapter. In particularly important sections of the book, this will involve reading the chapter a second time and stopping at each heading and * to think about (and to write a summary of) what you have just read.
4   Attempt the 'Source-based questions' section. It will sometimes be sufficient to think through your answers, but additional understanding will often be gained by forcing yourself to write them down.

When you have finished the main chapters of the book, study the 'Further Reading' section and decide what additional reading (if any) you will do on the topic.

This book has been designed to help make your studies both enjoyable and successful. If you can think of ways in which this could have been done more effectively, please write to tell me. In the meantime, I hope that you will gain greatly from your study of History.

Keith Randell

CHAPTER 1

Introduction: France in Revolution

1 Studying France in Revolution

The French Revolution is one of the most studied, most written about
and most exciting events in modern European History. It can also
appear to be one of the most complicated and confusing topics for the
student. So many important events were crammed into a period of only
13 years (1787–1799) and so many leading characters emerged only to
be rapidly eclipsed (and often eliminated) that bewilderment can
quickly follow one's initial contact with the subject. The best method of
avoiding this is to be reasonably self-disciplined in your studies.

The easiest way to do this is to design your own survival kit for the
topic. This needs to have three elements:

i)   An outline date chart to list the chronological stages into which the
topic is normally divided. This will provide you with a time-map
of the period and will allow you to place detailed events in a wider
context. You can build up your outline date chart from section 2 of
this chapter and from the summary chart on page 6. You will be
able to build up detailed time charts on each of the stages when
reading the rest of the book.

ii)   An historiographical outline to map out the main approaches that
have been adopted by historians in their research into the topic.
You can draw up your historiographical outline from reading the
remainder of this chapter. This outline should be used to place the
narratives that appear in subsequent chapters into a historiographical context.

iii)   A biographical list to contain the names of all the people who
appear in the book. For each person you should include sufficient
detail to remind you *when* and *why* he or she was of significance to
France in Revolution. The most efficient way to do this is to
compile an alphabetical list from the index. Write each name on a
separate line, leaving three clear lines between entries. You can
then add the details as you come across them in reading the book.
If you run out of space for any entry then further details can be
recorded on supplementary sheets, but this should not be necessary if you restrict yourself to 'headline' information.

Some people find that such a disciplined approach to study spoils the
enjoyment of discovering a new topic. If you feel that you would enjoy
initially finding out about the French Revolution without interrupting

the flow of your reading by stopping to write, there is much to be said in favour of reading the whole of this book as rapidly as possible without carrying out any of the suggested study activities, and then re-reading and completing the tasks that appear useful to you. Certainly, such a strategy should enable you to experience the freshness of a topic that has more intriguing ideas and events associated with it than almost any other.

2   The Marxist Interpretation

The dominant interpretation of the French Revolution for much of this century has been the Marxist interpretation. This was most clearly expressed nearly 60 years ago by the great French historian Georges Lefebvre, and later by his disciple Albert Soboul. Lefebvre regarded the French Revolution as a bourgeois revolution. The commercial and industrial bourgeoisie had been growing in importance in the eighteenth century and had become stronger economically than the nobility. Their economic strength was not, however, reflected in their position in society. They were kept out of positions of power by the privileged nobility and resented their inferior position. A class struggle therefore developed between the rising bourgeoisie and the declining aristocracy, whose poorer members clung to their privileges with desperate tenacity. The bourgeoisie were able to win this struggle because the monarchy became bankrupt owing to the cost of the wars in which it had fought, especially the American War of Independence.

At the outset, however, it was the privileged groups, the aristocracy and clergy, who joined forces to prevent the King's ministers from making any reforms which would reduce their privileges. It was they who began the first of the four revolutions that took place between 1787 and 1789. The aristocratic revolt was the first revolution. It was an attempt to secure for France a limited monarchy, in which real power would be held by the nobility. At first they had the support of the bourgeoisie in seeking to limit the power of the King and in calling for a representative body, the Estates-General. What ended the united opposition to the King was the decision in September 1788 that the Estates-General should meet as it had done in 1614, the last occasion it had been called. This meant that the aristocracy and clergy would be able to outvote the Third Estate, which represented the rest of the people, led by the bourgeoisie. So began the bourgeois revolution, a class struggle against the aristocracy, in which the bourgeoisie sought to destroy the privileges of the nobles and the Church. The French Revolution was above all, says Lefebvre, a struggle for equal rights. In this conflict the bourgeoisie needed the support of the population of Paris, as the King tried to use force to crush the second revolution. He was prevented by a popular rising in Paris, during which the Bastille fell in July 1789. This was the third revolution. A fourth revolution of the peasants also took place, largely as a result of the bad harvest of 1788, and this led to the King losing control of the countryside.

These revolutions were followed by widespread reforms from 1789–1791, when the institutions of the old regime were abolished and replaced by a new administrative structure, much of which still remains. However, the Revolution did not come to an end, because the King and the aristocracy did not accept what had happened. A turning point came when war was declared on Austria in 1792. The King and Queen were accused of intriguing with the enemy and this led to the fall of the monarchy and the execution of the King. The war also led to a three-fold crisis, from which it appeared that the Revolution would not survive. An economic crisis resulted from the printing of more and more paper money to pay for the war. This led to inflation and popular discontent. Conscription was decreed in order to provide soldiers: resistance to it caused civil war in the Vendée. The third crisis occurred when the war went badly and foreign armies invaded France. Lefebvre saw the Terror as a response to these crises. Desperate measures were needed and these included executing the enemies of the Republic.

The support of the *sans-culottes* (Parisian workers) was needed for a successful war effort, so many of their demands were granted. However, the interests of the bourgeois leaders of the Revolution and the *sans-culottes* were different. The former believed in *laissez-faire* – a market free from government interference – whereas the latter wanted control of prices. A clash was, therefore, inevitable, particularly as the bourgeoisie had no intention of allowing the *sans-culottes* to take control of the Revolution. Robespierre began to cut back the power of the *sans-culottes* and executed some of their leaders but it was after his fall that the class interests of the bourgeoisie were shown most clearly. All controls on prices were removed. As a result, there was massive inflation and in Germinal and Prairial, in 1795, the starving *sans-culottes* rose in despair. These risings were crushed and this marked the end of the *sans-culottes* as a political force during the Revolution.

The threat to the new government of the Directory now came from the monarchists. They staged a rising in Vendémiaire in 1795, which was crushed by the army. The army was called in again in 1797 to purge the elected Councils, after electoral gains by the monarchists. As the Directory began to lose control of the country and brigandage spread, the bourgeoisie turned to a strong man in the army to secure their gains from the Revolution. In the *coup d'état* of Brumaire in 1799 Napoleon brought the Revolution to an end.

The Marxist interpretation gained added strength from the study of history from below. Before the 1950s nearly all historians had looked at the French Revolution from above – from the point of view of those who dominated society, such as nobles and bourgeois. The ordinary people were seen as an undifferentiated mass, who reacted predictably (by rioting) to food shortages and who followed the political lead of the upper classes. They were not seen as having any ideas or institutions of their own. Lefebvre in 1924 was the first to show that the peasants were not a monolithic bloc but consisted of different groups whose interests were often opposed to one another. Landless peasants and sharecroppers, for example, were usually hostile to the large tenant farmers, whom they called the 'rural bourgeoisie'. The Revolution increased, rather than reduced, these differences.

Soboul did for the *sans-culottes* what Lefebvre had done for the peasants in *The Parisian Sans-culottes of the Year II* (1958). He was soon followed by George Rudé's *The Crowd in the French Revolution* (1959) and Richard Cobb's *The People's Armies* (in two volumes 1961 and 1963). These historians looked at the popular movement and rejected the common description of it as 'a mob'. They saw that it had its own institutions and its own ideas and attitudes, which were different from those of the bourgeois leaders of the Revolution. Soboul studied the clubs and revolutionary committees and showed how the *sans-culottes* made the Revolution more radical and why they were destroyed by the Terror they had done so much to create. According to the American historian Robert Darnton, his analysis 'still stands as the best explanation of the climactic phase of the Revolution'. Rudé studied the social groups which formed the 'crowd', whilst Cobb (who is not a Marxist) discussed the revolutionary armies of the popular movement. All these historians showed that the *sans-culottes* were a vital revolutionary force, particularly in the years 1792–4.

3   Revisionist Interpretations

This Marxist account of the Revolution was generally accepted until the attack in the 1960s of 'revisionist' (anti-Marxist) historians. Leading this attack was the English historian Alfred Cobban. He pointed out that the revolutionary bourgeoisie were not businessmen or merchants (i.e. capitalists) but were lawyers and other professional men, many of whom were office-holders. He showed that the capitalist bourgeoisie were not leaders of the Revolution and that they gained little from it. Far from leading to the triumph and extension of capitalism, the Revolution retarded the development of capitalism in France for a generation. In 1799 industry remained small-scale and most peasants aimed simply at subsistence farming, as they had done before the Revolution.

The American historian George V. Taylor denied that there was a class conflict between the nobility and bourgeoisie. He maintained that both groups before the Revolution shared the same values and invested in the same things, such as land and government offices, which could be bought. Other historians have argued that all rich bourgeois could buy offices, many of which conferred nobility, so what they wanted to do was join the nobility rather than get rid of it. Both nobles and rich bourgeois formed part of the same élite. The idea that the fortunes of nobles in the eighteenth century were declining compared with those of the bourgeoisie, has also been attacked. There were some poor nobles but the richest people in France, at the end of the eighteenth century as at the beginning, were nobles.

Revisionist historians maintain that the abolition of privilege and noble status did not significantly change the nature of the élite which ruled France. Birth was no longer important, but wealth was, so that in 1799 France was ruled by *notables*, whose wealth was based on land-owning. Both ex-nobles and bourgeoisie formed part of this élite, just as they had done before the Revolution.

Some revisionist historians have concentrated on the counter-revolution (the opposition to the Revolution), which sometimes took the form of open revolt. In doing so they have changed the way we look at the Revolution. They have shown that the counter-revolution had little to do with British agents or aristocratic plots. It was a widespread, lasting and popular movement, which covered large areas of France from 1793–1797 and helps to explain much of what happened during those years: repression, the Terror, the failure of constitutional government from 1794–7 and the need for a dictator in 1799.

4   Assessment

What, then, remains of the Marxist interpretation of the Revolution? A great deal, including the four-fold revolution of 1787–9, the account of the fall of the monarchy and the role played by the *sans-culottes* during the Revolution. Much of the revisionist criticism has been concerned with the origins of the Revolution and with its results. Here much of the Marxist interpretation has been abandoned. The idea that the Revolution was a class war of bourgeoisie versus aristocrats has had to be discarded, as has the idea that the Revolution led to the dominance of the capitalist bourgeoisie and the development of capitalism. Yet the Revolution *was* a bourgeois revolution, in that all the revolutionary leaders (certainly after 1791) were bourgeois and the bourgeoisie were the chief beneficiaries of the Revolution. They were the ones who bought most of the church lands which were sold, and who benefited from the increase in career opportunities open to talent, which enabled them to occupy all the high offices of state. They were not the only ones to benefit. All peasants who were landowners benefited by the abolition of feudal dues – about 4 million families or 18 million people out of a population of 28 million. So the Revolution was not the 'disaster' depicted by some revisionist historians. There is no end to the research on the French Revolution and to the controversies about its significance. What this short book tries to do is to acquaint you with the results of some of this research. Certainty is not to be expected, as many of the 'revisionist' positions described above are themselves now being criticised. The debate continues and is unlikely to end.

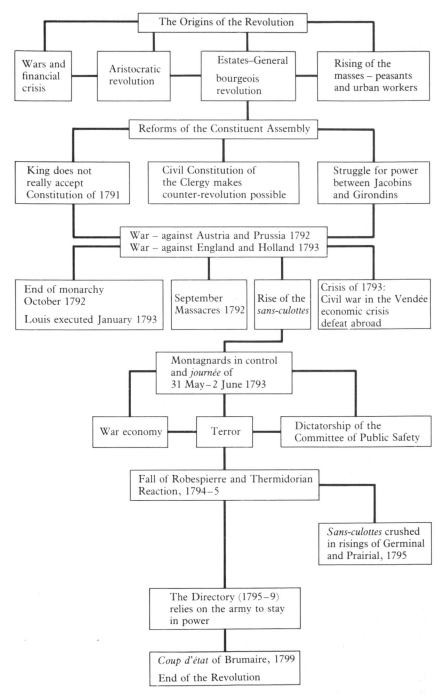

The Origins of the Revolution

Wars and financial crisis

Aristocratic revolution

Estates–General bourgeois revolution

Rising of the masses – peasants and urban workers

Reforms of the Constituent Assembly

King does not really accept Constitution of 1791

Civil Constitution of the Clergy makes counter-revolution possible

Struggle for power between Jacobins and Girondins

War – against Austria and Prussia 1792
War – against England and Holland 1793

End of monarchy October 1792

Louis executed January 1793

September Massacres 1792

Rise of the *sans-culottes*

Crisis of 1793:
Civil war in the Vendée economic crisis defeat abroad

Montagnards in control and *journée* of 31 May–2 June 1793

War economy

Terror

Dictatorship of the Committee of Public Safety

Fall of Robespierre and Thermidorian Reaction, 1794–5

Sans-culottes crushed in risings of Germinal and Prairial, 1795

The Directory (1795–9) relies on the army to stay in power

Coup d'état of Brumaire, 1799

End of the Revolution

Summary – France in Revolution

CHAPTER 2

The *Ancien Régime*

The '*ancien régime*' was an expression in common use by 1790 to describe the French system of government, laws and institutions which preceded the Revolution of 1789. An analysis of this society is necessary if we are to understand how the Revolution came about. It is also important to know what the administrative structure of France was like under the *ancien régime*, so that we can appreciate the extent of the changes which the Constituent Assembly brought about in 1789–91.

1 The King's Government

The kings of France were absolute in that their authority was not limited by any representative body, such as a parliament. They were responsible only to God. Louis XV expressed this view when he addressed the *Parlement* of Paris in 1766: 'sovereign power resides in my person alone . . . the power of legislation belongs to me alone – it is not dependent on or shared with anyone else.' The King could imprison anyone without bringing him to trial by issuing a *lettre de cachet* (the *cachet* was a wax seal). Yet the French monarchy was not despotic. To act in an arbitrary and illegal manner was to be despotic. The French King did not normally act in this way. He was bound by the laws and customs of his kingdom and there were many independent bodies, like the Assembly of the Clergy, which had rights and privileges which the King could not interfere with, as they were guaranteed by the law. The King made laws after consulting his councils, though he was not bound to accept their advice.

Considerable power was in the hands of a few ministers. The Controller-General was the most important of these, as he was in charge of the royal finances. There was no cabinet, where all the chief ministers could meet to make decisions in common. Nor was there a prime minister, as the King would never tolerate a minister whose power might rival his own.

In the provinces the King's government was carried on by the intendants 'of police, justice and finance'. They were appointed by and directly responsible to the King, who gave them wide powers in the 34 *généralités* (financial units) into which France was divided. They supervised the collection of taxes and the practice of religion. They also enforced law and order and were responsible for public works, communications, commerce and industry.

The main direct tax was the *taille*, a tax on commoners or land, which fell almost entirely on the peasants, owing to exemptions granted to towns and nobles. There were also the *capitation* (a poll tax) and the *vingtième* (a five per cent levy on all incomes). However, there was no uniformity in the incidence of these taxes. The Church did not pay them at all, and nobles did not pay the *taille*. Indirect taxes, which were levied on the goods people bought rather than on their incomes, could be a greater burden than direct taxes and brought in more money for the Crown. They included the *gabelle* (a tax on salt) which varied enormously from one part of France to another, *aides* on food and drink and the *octrois* on goods entering towns.

The French monarchy never received enough money from taxes to cover its expenditure, so it frequently had to borrow. Borrowing was especially heavy in wartime, when government expenses increased dramatically. As a result, payment of interest on the debt became an increasingly large part of government expenditure in the eighteenth century.

The chaotic method of tax collection ensured that the government did not receive anything like the full amount of taxes which were recovered. The Farmers-General collected the indirect taxes, paid a lump sum to the government in advance and kept for themselves anything above this that they could collect. Direct taxes were collected by hundreds of accountants, who often used the money for their own purposes. The accountants were venal office holders, who had bought their positions and could not be dismissed, as offices were regarded as a form of private property. On top of this, the lack of a central treasury into which all government revenues could be paid meant that the Controller-General never knew in any particular year how much money there was to spend.

There were several checks on the King's power. The most important of these were the privileges of corporate bodies, like the provincial estates and the *parlements*. The *pays d'états* (provincial estates) were areas on the periphery of France, like Brittany, which had been the last independent areas to be added to the French monarchy. They covered about half the kingdom and had ancient rights and privileges in justice and finance. For instance, they were exempt from paying some taxes. The provincial estates represented mainly the nobility and clung tenaciously to their privileges.

The *parlements* were other privileged bodies which limited the King's powers. They were law-courts – final courts of appeal in their respective areas. There were 13 of them, of which the *Parlement* of Paris was by far the most important, as its jurisdiction covered about a third of France. The 2300 magistrates who sat in the courts were all *noblesse de robe* (so-called because of the robes officials wore), as their offices conferred nobility. (They were some of the most important people in France. Nearly all intendants and councillors of state and a majority of the King's ministers came from the *parlements*.) Because the magistrates bought their positions they could not be dismissed, unless the King repaid them the purchase price of their office.

As well as their judicial functions, the *noblesse de robe* also had a political role. No law could be applied until it had been registered by each of the *parlements*. Before registering an edict the *parlement* could criticise it in a remonstrance sent to the King. If he wished, the King could ignore a remonstrance and insist, by what was known as a *lit de justice*, that the *parlement* register his edict. As the *parlements* opposed many of the royal edicts which aimed to change the system of taxation, nearly all historians up to the 1960s accused them of defending their own privileges and selfish interests when they claimed to be representing the nation and opposing 'ministerial despotism'. They were seen as the main obstacle in the way of a reforming monarchy. Recently some historians have taken a more sympathetic view of the *parlements*. They maintain that the *parlements* were defending the law and the rights of the people against the authoritarian monarchy.

The *pays d'états* and the *parlements* were part of the administrative confusion which prevailed in France under the *ancien régime*. As kings created new structures they did not abolish the old ones but simply added to them. In 1789 in France there were 35 provinces, 135 dioceses, 38 military regions and 34 *généralités*, as well as 13 *parlements*. None of these areas coincided with one another; all overlapped. There were different legal systems: Roman law in the south, various local laws in the north. France was also divided up into internal customs areas, so that goods moving from one part of France to another had to pay dues. There were various systems of weights and measures. There was therefore no uniform system of government which covered the whole of the country.

Some historians have seen the opposition of the *parlements* as the main reason why the King was unable to reform the financial system. In fact it was not the *parlements* that prevented the Crown from reforming but the character of the King. In France the King alone had the power to carry through reforms, so if the old regime did not reform it was the King's fault. Louis XVI was well-meaning and wanted to do what was best for France. He was a devout man and took seriously his duty, imposed by God, to rule in the interests of his subjects. Unfortunately he lacked self-confidence and drive. 'The weakness and indecision of the King', wrote the Comte de Provence, the elder of his two brothers, 'are beyond description'. It was his need for an older figure on whom he could lean that led Louis, on ascending the throne at the age of 20, to take Maurepas as his chief adviser. Maurepas was 73, had been out of office for 30 years and wanted a quiet life. He persuaded Louis to get rid of any minister who attempted reform or roused opposition. After Maurepas' death in 1781 Louis did not have a leading adviser but he remained as indecisive as ever. He had little knowledge of the country over which he ruled, or of its people. Only once before the Revolution did he move outside the Paris-Versailles area, to inspect a new harbour

Pre-revolutionary France

at Cherbourg. Louis was a clumsy and awkward figure in public. He did not inspire respect, although most Frenchmen looked on him with affection up to 1789.

This could not be said of the Queen. Marie Antoinette, the daughter of the Habsburg Empress, Maria Theresa, was a symbol of the unpopular alliance with Austria which had led to France's defeat in the Seven Years War (1756–63). She had the determination that Louis lacked but she was regarded as frivolous and arrogant. In one year she ran up gambling debts of half a million *livres* and was known as Madame Deficit by her brother-in-law, the Comte de Provence. She was hated by nearly everyone.

2 The Enlightenment

It was the passivity of the King rather than the strength of opposition which prevented reform. However, there was one movement in the late eighteenth century which made reform seem not only desirable but necessary. This was the Enlightenment. The *philosophes*, writers rather than philosophers, like Voltaire, Montesquieu and Rousseau, wrote on the problems of the day and attacked the prejudice and superstition they saw around them. Many of them contributed to the most important work of the French Enlightenment, *The Encyclopaedia* (the first volume appeared in 1752, the last of 35 in 1780). Their aim was to apply rational analysis to all activities. They were not prepared to accept tradition or revelation as a sufficient reason for doing anything. They were very much in favour of liberty – of the press, of speech, of trade, of freedom from arbitrary arrest – rather than equality, though they did want equality before the law. The main objects of their attack were the Church and despotic government. They did not accept the literal interpretation of the Bible and rejected anything which could not be explained by reason – miracles, for example – as superstitious. They condemned the Catholic Church because it was wealthy, corrupt and intolerant and took up Voltaire's cry of '*Écrasez l'infâme*' ('crush the infamous', meaning the Church).

The attack on despotism was mounted by Montesquieu in particular. His *Spirit of the Laws*, one of the most influential books in the eighteenth century, appeared in 1748. Monarchy, he said, was the government of one man according to the law: despotism the government of one man not restrained by law and was arbitrary. Under it no-one could feel secure. Montesquieu had been president of the *Parlement* of Bordeaux and he saw the *parlements* and the provincial estates as having a special role as intermediaries between the King and his subjects. Their power prevented the King becoming a despot. Not surprisingly, the *parlements* were enthusiastic about his ideas, whilst public opinion largely accepted the *parlements* as defenders of the rights of the people against 'ministerial despotism'.

The *philosophes* might criticise some institutions of the *ancien régime* but they were not opposed to the regime itself and they were not revolutionary. Many of them, including Montesquieu, were nobles and those who were not, like Voltaire and Rousseau, were accepted in high society.

*How important were the writings of the *philosophes* in forming a public opinion that was critical of the *ancien régime*? Did they help to bring about revolution? On issues like this historians have widely different views. Some think that although the *philosophes* were not revolutionary, the effect of their teaching was, as they attacked all the assumptions on which the *ancien régime* rested. By the 1780s much of France, at all social levels, was prepared for widespread changes and eager to bring them about. The Comte de Ségur commented:

1 We lent enthusiastic support to the philosophic doctrines professed by bold and witty scribblers. Voltaire won us over, Rousseau touched our hearts and we felt a secret pleasure when we saw them attack an old structure that appeared to us gothic and
5 ridiculous. So whatever our rank, our privileges, the remains of our former power eaten away beneath our feet, we enjoyed this little war. Untouched by it, we were mere onlookers. These battles . . . did not seem to us likely to affect the worldly superiority we enjoyed and which centuries-old possessions made
10 us believe indestructible . . . It can be pleasurable to sink so long as one believes one can rise again at will.

The ideas of Montesquieu were expressed in the remonstrances of the *parlements*. The French historian Chaussinand-Nogaret found that the *cahiers* (list of grievances) of the nobles in 1789 were steeped in the ideas of the Enlightenment. Their authors were deeply hostile to the *ancien régime* and anxious to create a state that was liberal and representative. On the other hand, the American historian G. V. Taylor did not find much influence of the Enlightenment in the *cahiers* of the Third Estate, which were very conservative. 'The only possible conclusion', he wrote, 'is that the revolutionary programme and its ideology were produced and perfected after the voters had deliberated in the spring [of 1789] and that the great majority of them neither foresaw nor intended what was about to be done'. Other historians have followed this line of thinking in maintaining that the influence of the Enlightenment came after the Revolution had begun and not before it. Only when the *ancien régime* had collapsed and new institutions had to be constructed did the ideas of the Enlightenment produce a revolutionary ideology. Joan McDonald claims that Rousseau's *Social Contract* 'did not play an important part in shaping the views of those who participated in the events of 1789. It was only after 1789 that interest in the *Social Contract* began to develop'.

3 French Society

French society in the eighteenth century was divided into orders or Estates. The First Estate was the clergy, the Second Estate was the nobility and the Third Estate was the rest of the population, made up of bourgeoisie, peasants and urban workers.

a) The First Estate

There were about 130 000 clergy. Of these 60 000 were members of religious orders (monks and nuns). The 70 000 secular clergy worked in the parishes. It was common for the youngest sons of the great noble families to enter the higher posts in the Church, so they could enjoy its vast wealth. The Archbishopric of Strasbourg was worth over 400 000 *livres* per annum (most *curés*, parish priests, received between 700 and 1000 *livres* per annum). Many bishops held more than one bishopric and never appeared in their sees at all. This was one of the great scandals which made the Church so unpopular.

The wealth of the Church came from the land it owned and from the tithes. It was the single largest landowner in France, owning about ten per cent of the land, although the proportion varied greatly from one area to another. In the north the Church held up to a third of the land, in Auverque only three per cent. The tithe was a proportion of each year's crop paid to the Church by landowners. Here again there was no uniformity. In parts of Dauphiné it was not much of a burden, as it amounted to only one fiftieth of the crop but in Brittany it was as much as a quarter. In most of France it was about seven to eight per cent of the crop. The tithe was supposed to provide for the local priest, poor relief and the upkeep of the church building, but most of it went instead to the bishops and abbots. It made a considerable contribution to the income of the higher clergy. This was greatly resented, by both lower clergy and peasants, as their *cahiers* showed in 1789.

The Church had many privileges apart from collecting the tithe. Its most important privilege and one which added to its unpopularity was its exemption from taxation. Instead of paying taxes, the Assembly of the Clergy, dominated by the bishops, negotiated with the King to make an annual payment to the Crown, known as a *don gratuit* or 'free gift'. It was always much less than they would have paid in normal taxation and was under five per cent of clerical income.

Catholicism was the state religion. The functions of the Church, however, extended far beyond the practice of religion. It had wide-ranging powers of censorship, provided poor relief, hospitals and schools and acted as a modern Registry Office by keeping a list in the parish registers of all births, marriages and deaths. It also acted as a sort of Ministry of Information, as the only way government policies became widely known was through the priests informing their congregations.

b) The Second Estate

The Second Estate was the most powerful. There have been widely differing estimates of the number of nobles, including their families, which range from 110 000 to 350 000 – between 0.5 per cent and 1.5 per cent of the population. Even if the lowest figure of 25 000 families is taken, this is over a hundred times larger than the British peerage (220 in 1790). The most powerful were the 4000 court nobility, restricted in theory to those whose noble ancestry went back before 1400; in practice to those who could afford the high cost of living at Versailles. Second in political importance were the *noblesse de robe*, the legal and administrative nobles, especially the magistrates of the *parlements*. The rest of the nobles, the majority, had never seen Versailles and lived in the country. As primogeniture ensured that their estates would be inherited by the oldest son, other sons, who also inherited noble status, had to find jobs in the Church, the army or the administration. But to buy an office was expensive and about a quarter of the nobility were too poor to do so. They had, therefore, either to enlist in the ranks or work their small estates themselves.

The main source of income for the Second Estate was land. The nobility owned between a quarter and a third of the land in France and between 15 per cent and 25 per cent of the Church's income went to them, as all the bishops were nobles. Nearly all the highest positions in the land were held by nobles. They were the King's ministers, his high legal officials, his intendants in the provinces, and they occupied all the highest ranks in the army. In his pamphlet 'What is the Third Estate?' The Abbé Sieyès wrote in 1789:

> 1 In one way or another, all the branches of the executive have been taken over by the caste that monopolises the Church, the judiciary and the army. A spirit of fellowship leads the nobles to favour one another over the rest of the nation. Their usurpation is
> 5 complete; they truly reign.

In addition to holding all the top jobs, nobles enjoyed many privileges. They were tried in special courts, and were exempt from military service, the *gabelle* and the *corvée* (forced labour on the roads). They received feudal (also known as seigneurial) dues (see page 18), had exclusive rights to hunting and fishing and in many areas the monopoly right (known as *banalités*) to operate mills, ovens and winepresses. They also benefited from tax exemptions. Until 1695 they did not pay direct taxes at all. Then the *capitation* was introduced and in 1749 the *vingtième*, though they managed to pay less than they should have done of these taxes. They were generally exempt from the most onerous tax of all, the *taille*. The provincial nobles were strongly attached to these privileges, as the loss of feudal dues could lead to a drop in their income of as much as 60 per cent in areas like Upper Brittany (the loss in other areas could be as little as 10 per cent). It was the less wealthy of the nobles who felt that if they were to lose their tax privileges and give up their seigneurial rights they would be ruined. They opposed change and clung to their privileges, as these were all they had to distinguish them from commoners.

*Historians up to the 1960s talked of an 'aristocratic reaction', by which the nobles sought to prevent bourgeois from becoming nobles and from acquiring high positions in the State. The 'Ségur Ordinance' of 1781, which said that no-one could become an officer in the army unless his family had been ennobled for four generations, is produced as evidence for this. Yet the Ordinance was to help the poor provincial nobility, for whom the army was the main source of employment, against the rich *anoblis* (those recently ennobled) who had been able to buy promotion in the army. It was a struggle between the rich and the poor members of the nobility.

There were no signs in the late eighteenth century that the nobility was becoming a closed caste. It was possible to become a noble either by direct grant of the King or by buying certain offices. There were 50 000 venal offices in the royal civil service which could be bought, sold and inherited like any other property. 12 000 of these were ennobling offices. In the eighteenth century 2200 families were ennobled by buying offices and 4300 by the direct grant of the King. Thus between a quarter and a third of all noble families in 1789 had been recently ennobled. The nobility was an open élite. Turgot recognised this in 1776 when he wrote about the ease with which nobility could be purchased:

1 There is no rich man who does not immediately become noble
   and as a result the body of noblemen includes all the rich men and
   the controversy over privileges is no longer a matter of distinguished families against commoners but a matter of rich against
5 poor.

This upward mobility is shown by the Farmers-General, usually regarded as the richest bourgeoisie. Between 1726 and 1791 90 per cent of them became nobles. This élite did not become less open as the eighteenth century advanced. Some of the sons of the oldest noble families were happy to marry daughters of wealthy bourgeoisie in order to enhance the family fortunes. A contemporary observer, Sénac de Meilhan, commented on this when he wrote:

1 Increasing numbers of alliances between families of magistrates,
   financiers and those of the greater nobility forged links which
   bound these various classes together . . . The children of financiers raised themselves to judicial honours and embraced the

5 highest offices and sometimes ministries. The riches of financiers
  became the resources of great families grown needy and matches
  proliferated between the most illustrious stock and the most
  opulent moneyed interests.

The idea of an 'aristocratic reaction' stems from the belief that the
economic strength of the nobles was declining, compared with that of
the economically dominant bourgeoisie. Recent research has shown
that this is false. Although nobles would suffer derogation (loss of their
nobility) if they took part in the activities of commoners such as retail
trade or manual work, iron-founding and mining were excluded from
this ban. Nobles became heavily involved in industries such as mining
and metallurgy and were also major investors in trading companies
(wholesale trade) and banking. As landlords they benefited from the
rise of rents, which increased in the late eighteenth century as a result of
population pressure. The American historian Robert Forster has shown
that the richest people in the Toulouse area were 20 noble families, who
doubled their income from land in the second half of the century. Other
local studies have confirmed this. In Paris in 1749 nearly all the people
with an income of over half a million *livres* were nobles. Even in major
industrial centres like Lyon nobles remained the wealthiest group.
Only in the thriving seaports on the Atlantic, like Bordeaux, were the
bourgeoisie wealthier than the local nobles and here the richest moved
up into the ranks of the nobility.

c) The Third Estate

The term bourgeoisie has no precise meaning but it is convenient to
indicate commoners who were not peasants or urban workers. The
bourgeoisie was certainly not a class in the Marxist sense of a group that
owns the means of production and lives by exploiting a wage-earning
proletariat. Some bourgeois involved in industry did this but most did
not. Among the wealthiest bourgeoisie were merchants, as French
overseas trade was the most dynamic sector of the economy, with the
volume of trade increasing by 440 per cent between 1715 and 1789.
Other bourgeois were financiers, landowners, members of the liberal
professions (doctors, writers), lawyers and civil servants, many of
whom were venal office-holders. The bourgeoisie owned 39 000 out of
the 50 000 venal offices. There were about 2.3 million bourgeoisie in
1789 (just over eight per cent of the population). This was a threefold
increase since 1700.

Historians who regarded the nobility as declining in wealth, saw the
bourgeoisie as rising and anxious to gain political power. As noble
privilege stood in its way, it was hostile to the nobility. This view has
largely been discredited. The bourgeoisie were certainly rising in the
eighteenth century, not only in numbers but also in wealth. Finance,

industry and banking accounted for 20 per cent of French private wealth in the 1780s and of this the bourgeoisie had a large share. Vast fortunes were made in the Atlantic ports of Bordeaux, La Rochelle and Nantes by the colonial trade with the West Indies. The remaining 80 per cent of French wealth came largely from *rentes* (interest from investments in government stock) and income from the land. The bourgeoisie held about a quarter of the land in France and often owned seigneurial rights too, as they were a form of property that could be bought by anyone. Local studies show that about 15 per cent of *seigneurs* were bourgeois.

Though the bourgeoisie were rising they were not opposed to the nobility and did not question the system of privileges, at least until 1788. They accepted noble values as their own and wished to share in the system of privilege by becoming ennobled. The *avocats* (lawyers) of Nuits in Burgundy declared as late as December, 1788:

1 The privileges of the nobility are truly their property. We will respect them all the more because we are not excluded from them and can acquire them . . . Why, then . . . think of destroying the source of emulation which guides our labours?

Most ennobling offices required two or three generations of holders before hereditary nobility was acquired. However, this delay could be avoided by the very wealthy. The slave trader, planter or financier could afford the high cost of an office such as King's Secretary, which conferred hereditary nobility directly. The merchants who made vast fortunes emulated the nobility by abandoning trade as soon as possible and put their money into land, office or *rentes*, as trade was regarded as ignoble and dishonourable. Bourgeoisie and nobles became part of a single, propertied élite. There was little bourgeois hostility to the nobility before 1788.

If the bourgeoisie was by far the wealthiest part of the Third Estate, the peasantry was by far the most numerous. About 85 per cent of the French population lived in the countryside and most of them were peasants. Estimates of the amount of the land they owned vary from 25–45 per cent of the total, though these figures disguise wide regional differences. There was a small group (perhaps 600 000) of large-scale farmers who grew for the market, employed other peasants as day labourers and loaned money. More numerous were the *laboureurs*, peasants who grew enough food to feed themselves and in a good year had a small surplus. For most of the eighteenth century they, and the big farmers, did well, as there were boom conditions until the 1770s. Although the majority of peasants had some land, it was not enough to live on. In order to survive they worked as day labourers and wove cloth in their homes. Half the peasants were share-croppers, who had no capital and gave half their produce to their landlords. About a quarter of all peasants were landless labourers, who owned nothing but their house and garden. Although serfdom had almost disappeared in France, there were still a million serfs in the east, mainly in Franche Comté. Their children could not inherit even their personal property without paying considerable dues to their lord. The poor peasant had no hope of improvement and lived in a chronic state of uncertainty. Bad weather or illness could push him into the ranks of the vagrants, who lived by begging, stealing and occasional employment.

All peasants had to pay tithe to the Church, taxes to the State and feudal dues to their lord. In the eighteenth century 'feudalism' meant the rights and privileges enjoyed by landlords and the dues and obligations owed to them by peasants. Nearly all land was subject to feudal dues. These included the *corvée*, *champart*, harvest dues and *lods et ventes* – a payment to the *seigneur* when property changed hands. A further grievance was that the peasant could be tried in the seigneurial court, where the lord acted as judge and jury. The incidence of all these dues varied considerably from one part of France to another. Peasants in the Midi paid hardly any feudal dues, whereas in Brittany and Burgundy they were heavy.

Taxes paid to the State included the *taille*, *vingtième*, *capitation* and *gabelle*. All these increased enormously between 1749 and the 1780s, in order to pay for the wars in which France became involved. Taxes took between five and ten per cent of the peasants' income.

The heaviest burden on the peasants was often not taxes, the tithe or feudal dues, but rents. These increased markedly in the second half of the eighteenth century as a result of the increase in population, which rose from 22.4 million in 1705 to 27.9 million in 1790.

The third part of the Third Estate was made up of urban workers. The majority of workers in the towns lived in crowded and insanitary tenements. They were unskilled and poor. Skilled craftsmen were organised in guilds. In Paris in 1776 they had 100 000 members, a third of the male population. Working hours were long – sixteen hours a day, six days a week. Workers were not allowed to combine to obtain higher wages or better working conditions. The standard of living of wage-earners had slowly fallen in the eighteenth century, as prices had risen on average by 65 per cent between 1726 and 1789, wages by only 22 per cent.

There was scarcely any large-scale production: the average number of people in the workshops of Paris in 1789 was 16. Masters and men worked and lived together and both were affected by a rise in the price of bread after a bad harvest, as bread formed three-quarters of most workers' diet. When prices rose they tended to seek a reduction in the price of bread rather than a rise in wages. Like the peasant in the countryside, they seized supplies in times of shortage and sold them at a 'fair' price.

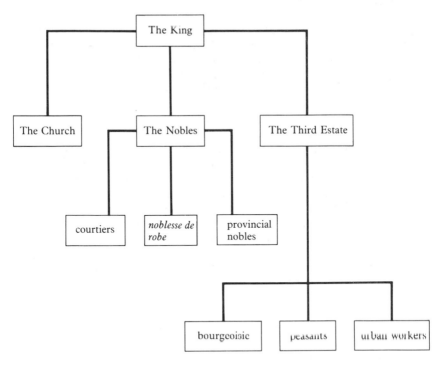

Summary – The Ancien Régime

Making notes on The Ancien Régime

Although you are unlikely to be asked direct questions on the *ancien régime*, a knowledge of it is essential when you write about the origins of the French Revolution or the changes the Revolution brought about. The following headings and sub-headings should ensure that you include the main points:

1.   The King's Government
1.1. The King's powers
1.2. Royal finances – direct and indirect taxes; method of collection; loans
1.3. Limits to the King's powers – *pays d'états; parlements*
1.4. Louis XVI and Marie Antoinette
2.   The Enlightenment. Did it help to bring about the Revolution?
3.   French Society

3.1. The First Estate – the Church
3.2. The Second Estate – the nobility
3.3. The Third Estate – bourgeoisie, peasants, urban workers. Was the bourgeoisie in conflict with the nobility?

Source-based questions on 'The Ancien Régime'

1   The Enlightenment
Read carefully the account by the Comte de Ségur on page 12. Answer the following questions:
a) Why do you think he 'lent enthusiastic support to the philosophic doctrines'?
b) Are there any indications in what he says that he would be likely to regret his 'support'?
c) What other evidence can you find to confirm or reject what Ségur says?

2   The Nobility
Read carefully the extracts from Sieyès (page 14), Turgot (page 15), Sénac de Meilhan (page 15), and the *avocats* of Nuits (page 17). Answer the following questions:
a) Did nobles 'favour one another over the rest of the nation', as Sieyès maintains?
b) In what ways did they 'truly reign'?
c) Were the nobility a closed caste?
d) What evidence is there in these extracts to show that the bourgeoisie were not hostile to the nobility?
e) Is this confirmed by what you know about the bourgeoisie?

CHAPTER 3

The Origins of the French Revolution

1 Introduction

Georges Lefebvre saw in the years 1787–1789 not one revolutionary movement but four. First came the revolution of the aristocracy, which sought to defend its privileges and even extend them. Through the *parlements* and the Assembly of Notables it resisted attempts by the Crown to reduce its taxation privileges. It was the aristocracy who demanded the calling of the Estates-General and it was this that led to the second revolution, that of the bourgeoisie. The bourgeoisie had supported the aristocracy in its opposition to 'ministerial despotism' until September 1788, when the *Parlement* of Paris said that the Estates-General should be formed as it was when it last met in 1614. This would mean that the two privileged orders would be able to outvote the Third Estate. The bourgeois leaders of the Third Estate would not accept this and so began a struggle against the aristocracy. They sought equality and this involved destroying the privileges of the nobility and the Church and setting up a system where promotion to high office was according to merit, not birth, where all paid taxes on the same basis and where the law was the same for all. The Revolution of 1789 was, above all else, the struggle for equal rights.

In its struggle against the King and the privileged orders – for the two had now combined to resist the bourgeois assault – the bourgeoisie needed the support of the Paris populace. In July the Crown attempted to use force to dissolve the National Assembly but was prevented from doing so by the rising of the *menu peuple*, the artisans and workers of Paris, which culminated in the fall of the Bastille. This saved the National Assembly and ensured the success of the Revolution. This third revolution, the popular revolution, arose from the economic crisis which had seen the price of bread rise to its highest point on the day the Bastille fell, 14 July 1789. Meanwhile, a fourth revolution, that of the peasants, was taking place. This had begun in the spring of 1789 and sought the abolition of seigneurial dues and labour services. Like the popular revolt, the peasant revolution resulted from the economic crisis and the bad harvest of 1788. The National Assembly attempted to bring it to an end with the August Decrees. In this chapter we shall be looking at how these four revolutions arose, how they developed and how they interacted with one another.

2 Financial Crisis and Aristocratic Revolt

On 20 August 1786, Calonne, the Controller-General, told Louis XVI that the government was on the verge of bankruptcy. Revenue for 1786 would be 475 million livres, expenditure 587 million livres, making a deficit of 112 million – almost a quarter of the total income.

Why was there a financial crisis in France? One reason is that between 1740 and 1783 France was at war for 20 years, first in the War of the Austrian Succession (1740–8), then the Seven Years War (1756–63) and finally the American War of Independence (1778–83). All these were immensely costly, especially the last one, and led the government to increase the national debt by borrowing on a large scale. This did not necessarily lead to revolution, however. Britain was also heavily in debt and her tax burden per head was three times heavier than in France. The difference was that in Britain the Parliament guaranteed loans, whereas in France there was no such representative body to give confidence to lenders.

This has led some historians to find the main reason for the crisis in the structure of the French financial system. The Crown was not receiving much of the money collected in taxes (see Chapter 2), and until it recovered control of its finances, no basic reforms could be carried out. The taxation privileges of the nobility and clergy also contributed to the problem. Yet, as their numbers were small and many were poor, their paying taxes on an equal basis with the rest of the population would not have significantly reduced the deficit.

a) Attempts at Reform

During the American War Jacques Necker, a Protestant banker from Geneva, was made Director-General of Finance because of his knowledge of the international money market and his ability to obtain loans with which to pay for the war. In this he was successful, but in order to persuade financiers to lend he had to pay a very high rate of interest. Necker has been attacked by historians in the past. It has been maintained that he financed the American War (France entered this on the side of the colonists in 1778) by borrowing huge sums of money. This increased the Crown's debts enormously, so that as much as 50 per cent of its income went to pay the interest on the debt. He did a further disservice to the Crown, it is argued, by publishing in 1781 the *Compte Rendu au Roi*, which showed a surplus when in fact there was a deficit. This was to be a millstone round the necks of future Controllers-General. They could no longer increase taxation in peacetime, because Necker had been seen to run a costly war without doing so.

This picture has been changed by the research of several historians, particularly that of J. F. Bosher in his *French Finances, 1770–1795*. Bosher regards Necker as 'the most determined of the reformers', as he began to tackle vigorously the heart of the problem and sought to gain control over the King's finances. He wanted to replace the independent, venal financiers by dependent, salaried officials, whom the Controller-General could appoint and dismiss. He succeeded in getting rid of 50 of the most powerful Receivers-General (accountants). He also took steps to establish a central Treasury, into which all taxes would be paid and from which all expenditures would be made.

In 1781 he issued the *Compte Rendu* to assure creditors that the interest on their loans was secure. This was the first public statement of the royal finances and it created a sensation. It carefully distinguished between ordinary peacetime expenditure and extraordinary wartime costs. Necker showed that there was a surplus of 10 million livres on the ordinary account. When he tried to bring the biggest spenders, the Ministers of War and the Marine, under his control and demanded a seat on the royal council, the other ministers threatened to resign. The King failed to support his reforming minister and Necker was dismissed.

After Necker there were six reactionary years from 1781–7. Finance Ministers, especially Calonne, undid much of his work by restoring noble, venal financiers to their previous positions. Both Joly de Fleury and Calonne borrowed much more heavily than Necker had done. Calonne had to offer 12–16 per cent interest to attract loans, as by the 1780s Britain, America and Russia were regarded as more secure places for investment than France. But in 1786, with loans drying up, he began a reform of the tax system. Calonne's main proposal was to replace the *capitation* and *vingtième* by a single land tax, payable by everyone including the nobles, the clergy and the *pays d'états*. This would by no means have solved the problem. It was estimated that it would bring in only 80 million livres, much less than the deficit expected for 1786, so further loans would still be required.

Calonne knew that the *parlements* would be likely to oppose his plans, so he persuaded the King to call an Assembly of Notables, which had last met in 1626, to give approval. The Assembly met in February 1787. Calonne did not expect much opposition, as the members had been chosen by the King. However, the King's choice was largely decided by precedent – thus the leading members of the *parlements*, princes, leading nobles and important bishops were selected. It was these people who immediately attacked Calonne's proposals. The clergy had most to lose, as they would have to pay taxes on the same basis as other people for the first time. The Notables asked for a statement of the Crown's income and expenditure so that they could judge the financial situation for themselves, and were angry when Calonne refused their request. They disliked the land tax because, unlike the *vingtième* it was to replace, it was for an indefinite number of years. The Notables were not opposed to all change and agreed that taxation should be on an equal basis, but they claimed that the approval of the nation was needed for Calonne's reforms and called for a meeting of the Estates-General, which had last met in 1614. Meanwhile the Notables rejected Calonne's proposals, heralding the revolt to come. Louis, realising the strength of opposition to Calonne, dismissed him in April 1787.

In calling the Notables the King had appeared to admit that he needed the consent of a national assembly for his reforms. Public opinion supported the Notables, who were seen as opponents of royal despotism. At this stage everyone seemed to be opposed to the King and his ministers.

★Calonne was replaced by one of the Notables, Loménie de Brienne, Archbishop of Toulouse, whilst another Notable, Lamoignon, President of the *Parlement* of Paris, became head of the Judiciary. As the Assembly of Notables was no more cooperative with Brienne than it had been with Calonne, its session was ended on 25 May. Brienne, like Necker, has been heavily criticised by historians as too easy-going to carry out the reforms that were needed. Bosher, however, has reversed the picture and he is now seen as one of the greatest reforming ministers of the century. He retained Calonne's land tax but also took up Necker's work and began an extensive programme of reform. There was to be an end to venal financial officials, a new central treasury established, laws codified, the educational system reformed, religious toleration introduced and the army made more efficient and less expensive. But Brienne now had to put his reforms before the *Parlement* of Paris for registration. The *Parlement* refused and said that only the Estates-General could consent to new taxes. Malesherbes, who had joined the ministry, said in June 1787:

1 The Parlement of Paris is, at this moment but the echo of the public of Paris and . . . the public of Paris is that of the entire Nation.

The popularity of the monarchy was declining rapidly, especially when the King exiled the *Parlement* to Troyes on 15 August.

The opposition of the Paris and provincial *parlements* paralysed the government, as it prevented the Crown from obtaining the money it needed. As a result the King gave way and in September allowed the *Parlement* to return to Paris. New taxation was abandoned and Brienne agreed to call the Estates-General before 1792. Arthur Young was acutely aware of the prevailing anxiety and confusion when he dined in Paris in October 1787:

1 One opinion pervaded the whole company, that they are on the eve of some great revolution [i.e. change] in the government: that everything points to it: the confusion in the finances great; with a deficit impossible to provide for without the states-general of the
5 kingdom, yet no ideas formed of what would be the consequence of their meeting . . . a great ferment amongst all ranks of men, who are eager for some change, without knowing what to look to, or to hope for: and a strong leaven of liberty, increasing every hour since the American revolution; . . . it is very remarkable that

10 such conversation never occurs but a bankruptcy is a topic: the curious question on which is, would a bankruptcy occasion a civil war and a total overthrow of the government?

On 3 May 1788 the *Parlement* appeared as the defender of the rights of the nation in proclaiming the 'fundamental laws' of the kingdom. It said that the right to vote taxes belonged solely to the Estates-General, that Frenchmen could not be imprisoned without trial and that the King could not change the privileges and customs of the provinces. As a result, Lamoignon decided to curtail drastically the powers of the *Parlement*. On 8 May 1788 the *parlements* were deprived of their right to register, and protest against, royal decrees. This would now be carried out by a new Plenary Court, whose members would be appointed by the King. The judicial powers of the *Parlement* were also reduced, as much of their work was given to other courts. Ministerial despotism had returned.

b) Aristocratic Revolt

The result of this high-handed action was the aristocratic revolt: the most violent opposition that the government had yet met. There were riots in some of the provincial capitals where the *parlements* met, such as Rennes in Brittany and Grenoble in Dauphiné. In all parts of the country nobles met in unauthorised assemblies to discuss action in favour of the *parlements*. An Assembly of the Clergy, too, joined in on the side of the *parlements*, breaking its long tradition of loyalty to the Crown. It condemned the reforms and voted a *don gratuit* of less than a quarter the size requested by the Crown.

How serious was all this opposition? It was restricted to a few places, which were far from Paris and from each other. The actions of those protesting were unco-ordinated. In Paris there was no popular support for the nobles' revolt. Had they been given time, the new courts would probably have worked effectively. It was likely that the trouble would have passed away, as it had done in the early 1770s, when the *Parlement* of Paris had been exiled and new courts set up.

What prevented this from happening was the collapse of the government's finances. Financiers were no longer willing to lend money to the government, owing to the economic crisis and Lamoignon's May edicts. At the beginning of August 1788 the royal treasury was empty. Brienne agreed that the Estates-General should meet on 1 May 1789 and he suspended payments from the royal treasury – the Crown was bankrupt. He realised that only one man could restore government credit and so he persuaded the King, who was reluctant, to recall Necker. Brienne then resigned, as did Lamoignon. Necker returned to office and made it clear that, apart from raising loans to allow the government to function, he would do nothing until the Estates-General had met. He abandoned the reforms of Lamoignon and recalled the Parlement. The King had been compelled, by the financial crisis and the opposition of the *parlements*, to abandon the reforms of his ministers and to accept the calling of a representative body, the Estates-General. Such a body would almost certainly seek to reduce the power of the King.

3   The Estates-General

When the Paris *Parlement* returned in September and declared that the Estates-General should meet as in 1614 it lost its popularity overnight. Up to this point the bourgeoisie had taken little part in political agitation, which had been led by the privileged classes – the nobles and the clergy in the *Parlement* and the Assembly of Notables. Now the bourgeois leaders of the Third Estate began to suspect that the privileged orders had opposed 'ministerial despotism' because they wanted power for themselves and not because they wanted justice for the nation as a whole. They now demanded double representation for the Third Estate (so that they would have as many representatives as the other two orders combined), and voting by head instead of by order. They knew that this would give them a majority, as many of the First Estate, who were poor parish priests, would support the Third Estate. What is surprising is that this agitation was organised by a political club, later called the Society of Thirty, although it had nearly 60 members. This club largely consisted of liberal nobles. Of its members only five were commoners. Its propaganda was so successful in arousing resentment against privilege that a Swiss observer, Mallet du Pan, wrote:

1 Public debate has assumed a different character. King, despotism and constitution have become only secondary questions. Now it is war between the Third Estate and the other two orders.

This hostility was reflected in a pamphlet 'What is the Third Estate?', written by the Abbé Sieyès and published in January 1789. In this he attacked the First and Second Estates, not royal despotism. He said that if the privileged orders refused to join the Third Estate in a common assembly, then the commons, who represented the over-whelming majority of the nation, should take direction of the nation's affairs into its own hands.

In December 1788 the King's Council allowed the doubling of Third Estate deputies. Nothing was said about voting by head, so that when the Estates-General met there was bound to be confusion, the Third Estate assuming that there would be voting by head (otherwise doubling served no purpose) while the first two Estates assumed that there would not.

All the adult male members of the two privileged orders had a vote for electing their deputies. The Third Estate deputies were to be chosen by a complicated system of indirect election. Frenchmen over the age of 25 could vote in their primary assembly, either of their parish or their urban guild, if they paid taxes. They chose representatives who in turn elected the deputies.

Before the meeting of the Estates-General the electors of each of the three orders drew up *cahiers*, lists of grievances and suggestions for reform. Those of the First Estate reflected the interests of the parish clergy. They called for an end to bishops holding more than one diocese, and for those who were not noble to be able to become bishops. In return they were prepared to give up the financial privileges of the Church. They were not, however, prepared to give up the dominant position of the Church: Catholicism should remain the established religion and retain control of education. They did not intend to tolerate Protestantism.

The noble *cahiers* were surprisingly liberal – 89 per cent were prepared to give up their financial privileges and nearly 39 per cent supported voting by head, at least on matters of general interest. Instead of trying to preserve their own privileges, they showed a desire for change and were prepared to admit that merit rather than birth should be the key to high office. They attacked the goverment for its despotism, its inefficiency and its injustice. On many issues they were more liberal than the Third Estate.

Cahiers de Doléances	Percentage of the Nobility in favour	Percentage of the Third Estate in favour
Equality before the law	23	17
Abolition of *lettres de cachet*	68	74
Insistence on the establishment of a constitution as a precondition of any further grant of taxation	64	57
Division of legislative power between the King and the Estates-General	52	36
Giving legislative power to the Estates-General only	14	20
Regular meetings of the Estates-General	90	84

Cahiers de Doléances	Percentage of the Nobility in favour	Percentage of the Third Estate in favour
Control of taxation to the Estates-General	81	82
Fiscal equality	88	86
Ministerial responsibility to the Estates-General	73	74
A constitutional regime in general	62	49
Liberty of the press	88	74
Freedom of commerce	35	42
Abolition of monopolies	59	72
More economic freedom in general	45	66
Abolition of seigneurial rights	14	64

The parish *cahiers* of the Third Estate accurately reflected the wishes of the peasants, who wanted not only financial equality but also regulation of the grain trade and an end to the tithe and seigneurial rights. However, when these were taken to form part of the general *cahiers* of the Third Estate, the bourgeoisie, who drew these up, tended to leave out popular demands which they did not like. Like those of the other two orders the *cahiers* of the Third Estate called for regular meetings of the Estates-General, for civil liberties and provincial estates, for no taxation without consent and for equality of taxation. They also requested voting by head and careers open to talent. In addition, they were markedly more liberal than the noble *cahiers* in their desire for a more market-oriented economy.

The *cahiers* of all three orders had a great deal in common. All were against absolute royal power and all wanted a King whose powers would be limited by an elected assembly, which would have the right to vote taxes and pass laws. Only one major issue separated the Third Estate from the other two orders – voting by head. It was this that was to cause conflict when the Estates-General met.

*The government did not make any attempt to influence the elections to the Estates-General and had no candidates. The clergy overwhelmingly elected parish priests: only 51 of the 303 deputies were bishops. The majority of noble deputies were from old noble families in the provinces, many of them poor and conservative, but 90 out of the 282 could be classed as liberals and these were to play a leading role in the Estates-General. The 610 deputies elected to represent the Third Estate were educated, articulate and almost entirely well-off, largely because deputies were expected to pay their own expenses. This was something peasants and artisans could not afford. Not a single peasant or urban worker was elected. The largest group of Third Estate deputies were venal office holders (43 per cent), followed by lawyers (25 per cent), although two-thirds of deputies had some legal qualification. Only 13 per cent were from trade and industry. The industrial middle class did not play a leading role in events leading to the Revolution or, indeed, in the Revolution itself.

When the Estates-General met on 5 May 1789 the government had the opportunity to take control of the situation. The Third Estate deputies, lacking experience and having no recognised leaders, would have supported the King if he had promised reforms, but the government did not take the initiative and it put forward no programme. Necker talked about equality of taxation but did not mention any other reform. Nothing was said about a constitution, which all the *cahiers* had demanded.

Although the Estates-General met in three separate groups, the Third Estate insisted that the credentials of those who claimed to have been elected should be verified in a common session. This appeared a trivial matter but was seen by everyone as deciding whether the Estates-General should meet as one body (and vote by head) when discussing all other matters. The nobles rejected the Third Estate's demand and declared themselves a separate order by 188 votes to 46, as did the clergy but with a slender majority of 19. The Third Estate refused to do anything until the other two orders joined them, so weeks of paralysis followed, with the government failing to provide any leadership. Finally, on 10 June, the deadlock was broken when the Third Estate passed a motion that verification should begin, even if the other two orders did not accept their invitation to verify credentials in common. A trickle of priests joined the Third Estate in the following days, which on 17 June voted by 491 to 90 to call itself the National Assembly. The Third Estate was now claiming that, as it represented most of the nation, it had the right to manage its affairs and decide taxation. Events were rapidly moving out of the control of the government, especially when on 19 June the clergy voted to join the Third Estate.

*All this was a direct challenge to the authority of the King, who was at last forced to act. He decided to hold a Royal Session, attended by all three Estates, on 23 June, when he would propose a series of reforms. On 20 June the deputies of the Third Estate found that the hall in which they met had been closed to prepare for the Royal Session. They had not been informed and were furious. They met instead in a tennis court nearby and took an oath, known as the Tennis Court Oath, not to disperse until they had given France a constitution, thus claiming that the King had not the right to dissolve them. Only one member voted against the motion; 90 had voted against a motion to call themselves the National Assembly only three days before, so the deputies were rapidly becoming more radical.

It was Necker's idea to hold a Royal Session, where he hoped the King would ignore the events of 10–17 June and would accept voting in common on all important matters. Louis, under pressure from the Queen and his brothers, ignored this advice and came down very firmly on the side of the privileged orders. He declared null and void the decisions taken by the deputies of the Third Estate on 17 June. He would not allow the privileges of the nobility and clergy to be discussed in common. He was, however, prepared to accept considerable restrictions on his own power. No taxes would be imposed 'without the consent of the representatives of the nation', *lettres de cachet* would be abolished and freedom of the press introduced. Internal customs barriers, the *gabelle* and *corvée* were to be abolished. If these reforms had been put forward in May, a majority of the Third Estate would probably have been satisfied but now they did not go far enough. The King ended by ordering the deputies to disperse and meet in their separate assemblies.

The next day 151 clergy joined the Third Estate. The day after that 47 nobles, including a royal prince (the Duc d'Orléans) did the same. There were popular demonstrations in Paris in favour of the Assembly. On 27 June the King gave way. He reversed his decision of 23 June and ordered the nobles and clergy to join the Third Estate and vote by head. Arthur Young wrote on the 27th: 'The whole business now seems over and the revolution complete'. There was rejoicing in Paris. In the Assembly it looked as though all three orders were prepared to work harmoniously together and that Arthur Young was right. Yet he did not believe that the court would 'sit to have their hands tied behind them'.

Was the King prepared to accept what had happened or was he simply trying to buy time, so that he could call up troops to crush the Assembly? He had given the first orders to bring up troops to Paris and Versailles on 22 June. By late June nearly 4000 troops, including 2600 in foreign-speaking units, were stationed round Paris. This caused alarm in the capital. Government claims that they were there simply to preserve order seemed to have been sincere – until the last week in June. On 26 June, 4800 extra troops were ordered into the Paris region and on 1 July, 11 500 more. In less than a week the strength of army units called to Paris increased from under 4000 to over 20 000. It was impossible to doubt any longer that the King and his advisers had decided to dissolve the National Assembly, by force if necessary. In this desperate situation the Assembly was saved by the revolt of the people of Paris.

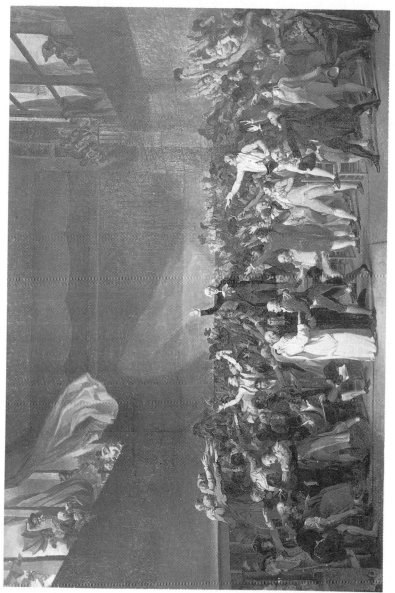

The Tennis Court Oath, by Jacques-Louis David

4   The Economic Crisis

In the late 1770s a depression began which affected the whole economy, apart from the colonial trade. Wine prices collapsed because of overproduction. This was disastrous for many peasants, for whom wine was an important cash crop. Poor harvests happened more frequently – in 1778–9, 1781–2 and 1785–6. In 1788 there was a major disaster, when the harvest was very poor. A bad harvest in a pre-industrial society always led to massive unemployment, as the resulting rise in the price of food led to less demand for manufactured goods, at a time when both peasants and urban workers needed employment more than ever to cope with the higher prices. Textiles, which accounted for half of industrial production, were particularly badly hit. They were already affected by the Eden Treaty of 1786, which came into operation in May 1787 and allowed imports of English goods, including textiles, at reduced import duties. Production and employment in the textile industries fell by 50 per cent in 1789.

In normal times a worker spent up to 50 per cent of his income on bread. In August 1788 the price of bread began to rise in Paris and by February 1789 it had gone up by over 50 per cent. By the spring of 1789 a Paris worker could be spending 88 per cent of his wages on bread. On 28 April the house and factory of a prosperous wallpaper manufacturer, Réveillon, were set on fire, as it was rumoured that he was going to reduce wages. But this riot was more a violent protest against the scarcity and high price of bread than a protest against wages. At least 50 people were killed or wounded by troops. The situation was therefore very volatile when the Estates-General met. Economic issues (the price of bread and employment) were, for the first time, pushing France towards revolution, and had created discontent which could be used by political groups to bring crowds on to the streets to save the National Assembly.

5   The Revolt of Paris

In late June, journalists and followers of the Duc d'Orléans established a permanent headquarters in the Palais Royal in Paris. Here thousands gathered each night to listen to revolutionary speakers. It was the Palais Royal that directed the popular movement.

By 11 July Louis had about 30 000 troops round Paris and Versailles and felt strong enough to dismiss Necker, who was at the height of his popularity and regarded as the people's chief supporter in the government. The deputies, alarmed, thought that Louis would dissolve the Assembly and arrest its leading members. When news of Necker's dismissal reached Paris the next day, Parisians flocked to the Palais Royal, where speakers called on them to take up arms. A frantic search began for muskets and ammunition. On the same day crowds of poor

Parisians attacked the hated customs posts, which surrounded Paris and imposed duties on goods, including food, entering the city. Out of 54 posts, 40 were destroyed. This action had not been planned but it frightened the respectable citizens of Paris, who feared that attacks on property and looting would follow. To gain control of the situation and prevent the indiscriminate arming of the population the Paris electors (representatives of the 60 electoral districts who had chosen the deputies to the Estates-General) set up a committee to act as a government of the city. They formed a National Guard or citizens' militia, from which most workers would be excluded. It had the double purpose of protecting property against the attacks of the *menu peuple* and of defending Paris against any possible attack by royal troops. It was these electors and the supporters of the Duc d'Orléans who were to turn what had begun as spontaneous riots into a general rising.

a) The Fall of the Bastille

The Parisians needed arms, so they went to the Invalides, an old soldiers' retirement home which also served as an arsenal, where they seized over 28 000 muskets and 20 cannon. They were still short of gunpowder and cartridges, so they marched on the fortress of the Bastille. The government could have used its troops to crush the rising but they proved unreliable. By late June many French Guards, who worked at various trades in Paris in their off-duty hours and mixed with the population, were being influenced by agitators at the Palais Royal. Discipline in this élite unit deteriorated rapidly. As early as 24 June two companies had refused to go on duty. By 14 July, 5 out of 6 battalions of French Guards had deserted and some joined the Parisians besieging the Bastille. There were 5000 other troops nearby, but the officers told their commander that they could not rely on their men. Troops were removed from the streets of Paris to the Champ de Mars on the outskirts, where they did nothing. The Parisians besieging the Bastille did not intend to storm it but when they had managed to enter the inner courtyard the governor, de Launay, who had refused to hand over the gunpowder, ordered his troops to fire. Of those laying siege 98 were killed before the French Guards, using cannon taken from the Invalides that morning, broke in. De Launay, forced to surrender, was murdered and decapitated. Those who had taken part in the attack on the Bastille were not wealthy middle class but *sans-culottes* – master craftsmen, journeymen and labourers of the working class districts. At the height of the rebellion about a quarter of a million Parisians were under arms.

*The events of 14 July had far-reaching results. The King had lost control of Paris, where the electors set up a Commune to run the city and made Lafayette commander of the National Guard. The Assembly (which on 7 July had taken the name of the National Constituent Assembly) could now begin to draw up a constitution safe from the threat of being dissolved by the King. Real power had passed from the King to the elected representatives of the people. Louis was no longer in a position to dictate to the Assembly, because he could not rely upon the army. Some historians see this as crucial for the success of the Revolution. Once the King had lost control of his armed forces, the Revolution was secure. When news of the fall of the Bastille spread through France, the peasant revolution, which had already begun, was extended and intensified. The revolt of Paris also led to the emigration of some nobles, led by the King's brother the Comte d'Artois: 20 000 fled abroad in two months.

On 17 July the King journeyed to Paris, where the people gave him a hostile reception. Louis recognised the new revolutionary council – the Commune – and the National Guard, and wore in his hat the red, white and blue cockade of the Revolution (red and blue were the colours of Paris, white of the Bourbons). The significance of the King's humiliation was not lost on foreign diplomats. The British ambassador, the Duke of Dorset, wrote:

1 the greatest Revolution that we know anything of has been effected with . . . the loss of very few lives: from this moment we may consider France as a free country; the King a limited monarch and the nobility as reduced to a level with the rest of the 5 nation.

Gouverneur Morris, later the US ambassador to France, told George Washington: 'You may consider the revolution to be over, since the authority of the King and the nobles has been utterly destroyed'.

b) The Municipal Revolution

One further result of the revolt of Paris was what became known as the municipal revolution. The authority of the King collapsed in most French towns, as it had done in Paris: his orders would now be obeyed only if they had been approved by the Constituent Assembly. Citizens' militias were set up in several towns, such as Marseille, before the National Guard was formed in Paris, and in some other towns revolutionaries seized power before they did so in the capital. However, most provincial towns waited to hear what had happened in Paris before they acted and this could take up to a fortnight. 'The Parisian spirit of commotion', wrote Arthur Young from Strasbourg on 21 July, 'spreads quickly'. Nearly everywhere there was a municipal revolution in which the bourgeoisie played a leading part. This took various forms. In some towns the old council merely broadened its membership and carried on as before. In Bordeaux the electors of the Third Estate seized control, closely following the example of Paris. In most towns, including Lille, Rouen and Lyon the old municipal corporations were overthrown by force. In nearly every town a National Guard was formed which, as in Paris, was designed both to control popular violence and to prevent counter-revolution. Nearly all intendants abandoned their posts. The King had lost control of Paris and of the provincial towns. He was to lose control of the countryside through the peasant revolution.

6   The Peasant Revolution

a) The Rural Revolt and the Great Fear

The peasants played no part in the events which led up to revolution until the spring of 1789. It was the consequences of the bad harvest of 1788 which gave them a role, because of the great misery and hardship in the countryside. Most peasants did not have enough land to provide for their needs and had to buy their bread. They were therefore badly affected by the rise in the price of bread in the spring and summer of 1789. Many suffered too from the unemployment in the textile industry, as they wove cloth in order to survive. From January 1789 grain convoys and the premises of suspected hoarders were attacked. This was normal in times of dearth and would probably have died out when the new crop was harvested in the summer.

What made these food riots more important than usual were the political events which were taking place. The calling of the Estates-General aroused general excitement amongst the peasants. They believed that the King would not have asked them to state their grievances in the *cahiers* if he did not intend to do something about them. The lieutenant-general of the Saumur district commented:

1 What is really tiresome is that these [electoral] assemblies . . .
  have generally believed themselves invested with some sovereign
  authority and that when they came to an end, the peasants went
  home with the idea that henceforward they were free from tithes,
5 hunting prohibitions and the payment of seigneurial dues.

They thought that if they anticipated what the King would do by, for example, burning the *terriers*, which listed peasant obligations, they would simply be carrying out his will. The fall of the Bastille also had a tremendous effect in the countryside. Risings immediately followed in Normandy and Franche Comté. Demonstrations and riots against taxes, the tithe and feudal dues spread throughout the country, so that it appeared that law and order had collapsed everywhere.

On the great estates of the Church and other landowners were storehouses of grain, which had been collected as rents, feudal dues and tithes. In the spring and summer of 1789 they were the only places where grain was held in bulk. It was not surprising, therefore, that landlords were regarded as hoarders and their *châteaux* were attacked.

They were attacked too because that is where the *terriers* were kept. On 28 June the President of the Grenoble *parlement* wrote:

> 1 There is daily talk of attacking the nobility, of setting fire to their *châteaux* in order to burn all their title-deeds . . . In *cantons* where unrest has been less sensational, the inhabitants meet daily to pass resolutions that they will pay no more rent or other seigneurial
> 5 dues but fix a moderate price for their redemption and lower the rate of the *lods*; endless hostile projects spring from that spirit of equality and independence which prevails in men's minds today.

Hundreds of *châteaux* were ransacked and many were set on fire but there was remarkably little bloodshed – landowners or their agents were killed only when they resisted.

The attack on the *châteaux*, inspired by the events in Paris, was caught up in what became known as the Great Fear, which lasted from 20 July to 6 August 1789. It began in local rumours that bands of brigands, in the pay of the aristocracy, were going to destroy the harvest. The peasants took up arms to await the brigands and when they did not appear, turned their anger against the landlords. The Great Fear spread the peasant rising throughout most of France, except for some areas on the periphery, such as Brittany, Alsace and the Basque region, which were unaffected.

b) The August Decrees

The Assembly was in a dilemma. It could not ask the King's troops to crush the peasants, because afterwards they might be turned against the Assembly itself. Yet they could not allow the anarchy in the countryside to continue. This could be ended and the support of the peasants gained for the Assembly and for the Revolution, by giving them at least part of what they wanted. On 3 August leaders of the 'patriot' party drew up a plan for liberal nobles to propose the dismantling of the feudal system. On the night of 4 August the Vicomte de Noailles, followed by the Duc d' Auguillon, one of the richest landowners in France, proposed that obligations concerned with personal servitude should be abolished without compensation: these included serfdom and the *corvée*. Other rights such as *champart* and *lods et ventes* were regarded as a form of property and were to be redeemed (paid for by the peasant). But these were the dues which affected the peasant most severely, so there was little satisfaction in the countryside with the limited nature of the reforms. These proposals were given legal form in the decrees of 5–11 August, which began:

> 1 The National Assembly abolishes the feudal system entirely. It decrees that, as regards feudal rights and dues . . . those relating

... to personal serfdom ... are abolished without compensation; all the others are declared to be redeemable and the rate and mode
5 of redemption will be determined by the National Assembly. Those of the aforementioned rights which are not abolished by this decree will continue to be collected until their owners have been compensated.

All seigneurial courts are abolished without any compensation.

Amid great excitement, the example of Noailles and Aiguillon was followed by other noble deputies, who queued up to renounce their privileges in a spirit of patriotic fervour. The changes proposed went far beyond what had been proposed in the *cahiers*.

1 All forms of tithe ... are abolished, subject to making alternative provision for the expenses of divine worship, payment of priests, poor relief etc. ... to which they are at present allocated.

Venality of judicial and municipal offices is abolished with
5 immediate effect. Justice will be administered without charge.

Financial privileges, whether relating to persons or to land, in matters of taxation are abolished for all time. Payment will fall on all citizens and all lands, in the same manner ...

Since a national constitution and public liberty are more advan-
10 tageous to the provinces than the privileges which some of them enjoy and which must be sacrificed for the sake of the intimate union of all the parts of the empire, it is declared that all the special privileges of the provinces, principalities, *pays*, *cantons*, towns and village communes, are abolished forever and assimi-
15 lated into the common rights of all Frenchmen.

All citizens, without distinction of birth, are eligible for all offices and dignities, whether ecclesiastical, civil or military.

When the Assembly adjourned at 2 am on 5 August the deputies were weeping for joy. 'What a nation! What glory. What honour to the French!' exclaimed Duquesnoy. Bailly, the Mayor of Paris, in his account of the session, stressed the revolutionary nature of the decrees:

1 Never before have so many bodies and individuals voted such sacrifices at one time, in such generous terms and with such unanimity. This has been a night for destruction and for public happiness. We may view this moment as the dawn of a new
5 revolution, when all the burdens weighing on the people were abolished and France was truly reborn. The feudal regime which had oppressed the people for centuries was demolished at a stroke

and in an instant. The National Assembly achieved more for the people in a few hours than the wisest and most enlightened
10 nations had done for many centuries.

*How important, then, were the August Decrees? They marked the end of noble power and the privilege of birth by establishing a society based on civil equality. Now all Frenchmen had the same rights and duties, could enter any profession according to their ability and would pay the same taxes. Of course, equality in theory was different from equality in practice. The career open to talent benefited the bourgeoisie rather than the peasant or worker, as the latter did not have the education to take advantage of it. Nevertheless, French society would never be the same again – the old society of orders had gone.

Another result of the August Decrees was the commitment of the peasants – the vast mass of the population – to the new regime, at least in so far as it removed their feudal obligations. They did not like having to redeem some of their feudal dues and many stopped paying them until they were finally abolished, without compensation, in 1793. Some, in areas like Brittany and the Vendée, were to become active opponents of the Revolution (see Chapter 5), but for most of them the Revolution marked the end of the feudal system and they feared that if they did not support it, aristocratic privilege and the tithe would return and they would lose all they had gained.

The August Decrees had swept away institutions like the provincial estates and cleared the way for a national, uniform system of administration. As most institutions had been based on privilege the Assembly now had to begin the long and laborious task, which would take two years to complete, of changing those concerned with local government, law, finance, the Church (whose income was halved by the loss of the tithe, so that it could no longer carry the burden of funding education, hospitals and poor relief), and the armed forces. Yet many thought that those who had lost power would try to recover it. There was a widespread fear of an aristocratic plot and a feeling that, without constant vigilance, the victories of July and August could be quickly reversed.

Making notes on 'The Origins of the French Revolution'

Your notes should help you to understand why there was a revolution in France in 1789. At each stage of the argument you should ask yourself three questions: Why did an event occur? What is its significance? How does it link up with other events? The following headings and sub-headings should provide a suitable framework for your notes:

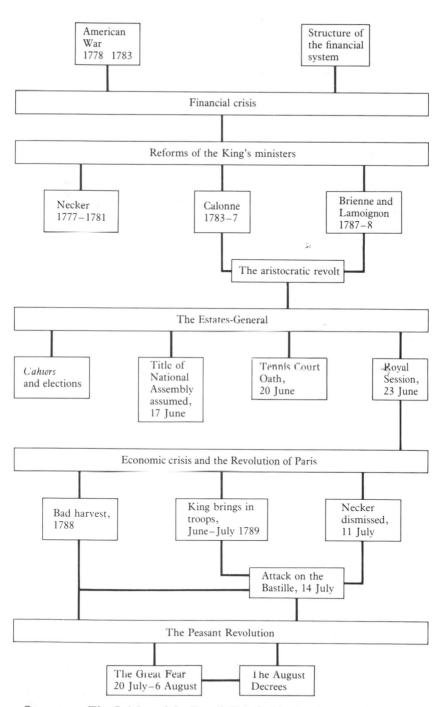

```
┌─────────────┐                              ┌─────────────┐
│ American    │                              │ Structure of│
│ War         │                              │ the financial│
│ 1778  1783  │                              │ system      │
└─────────────┘                              └─────────────┘
```

Financial crisis

Reforms of the King's ministers

```
┌─────────────┐          ┌─────────────┐    ┌─────────────┐
│ Necker      │          │ Calonne     │    │ Brienne and │
│ 1777–1781   │          │ 1783–7      │    │ Lamoignon   │
│             │          │             │    │ 1787–8      │
└─────────────┘          └─────────────┘    └─────────────┘
```

The aristocratic revolt

The Estates-General

```
┌─────────────┐  ┌─────────────┐  ┌─────────────┐  ┌─────────────┐
│ Cahiers     │  │ Title of    │  │ Tennis Court│  │ Royal       │
│ and elections│  │ National    │  │ Oath,       │  │ Session,    │
│             │  │ Assembly    │  │ 20 June     │  │ 23 June     │
│             │  │ assumed,    │  │             │  │             │
│             │  │ 17 June     │  │             │  │             │
└─────────────┘  └─────────────┘  └─────────────┘  └─────────────┘
```

Economic crisis and the Revolution of Paris

```
┌─────────────┐  ┌─────────────┐  ┌─────────────┐
│ Bad harvest,│  │ King brings in│ │ Necker      │
│ 1788        │  │ troops,     │  │ dismissed,  │
│             │  │ June–July 1789│ │ 11 July     │
└─────────────┘  └─────────────┘  └─────────────┘
```

Attack on the Bastille, 14 July

The Peasant Revolution

```
┌─────────────┐  ┌─────────────┐
│ The Great Fear│ │ The August  │
│ 20 July–6 August│ │ Decrees    │
└─────────────┘  └─────────────┘
```

Summary – The Origins of the French Revolution

1.   Financial Crisis and Aristocratic Revolt
1.1. The nature of the problem: war and the structure of the financial system
1.2. Attempts at reform: Necker, Calonne, Brienne and Lamoignon
1.3. The Aristocratic Revolt
1.4. The King gives way. What does he do?
2.   The Estates-General
2.1. The *cahiers* of the clergy, nobility and Third Estate
2.2. The elections – who represented each Estate?
2.3. May–June 1789. Note what happened on and the significance of:
      a) 17 June – the National Assembly
      b) 20 June – the Tennis Court Oath
      c) 23 June – the Royal Session
      d) 27 June – the King orders all the Estates to meet together
3.   The Economic Crisis
3.1. The bad harvest of 1788
3.2. Unrest in Paris – the Réveillon riots
4.   The Revolt of Paris
4.1. The King brings in troops around Paris
4.2. 11 July – Necker dismissed
4.3. 14 July – fall of the Bastille: what were the results of this?
4.4. The municipal revolution
5.   The Peasant Revolution
5.1. The nature of peasant discontent
5.2. The effect on the peasant of political events – the calling of the Estates-General, the *cahiers* and the fall of the Bastille
5.3. The Great Fear
5.4. The August Decrees – how and why do they go far beyond the demands in the *cahiers*?

Answering essay questions on 'The Origins of the French Revolution'

Examiners are not interested in a lot of facts put down in chronological order in an essay. They are looking for understanding and want to see if you can analyse events, see their importance and the connections of one with another. Questions are frequently of the 'Why?' type, or may take the form of a quotation, which you are asked to discuss. Remember that you are not necessarily expected to agree with a quotation. Questions on the causes of the Revolution tend to fall into three groups:

1. The social groups or classes which wanted a revolution.
2. The political, economic or financial origins of the Revolution.
3. The role of the monarchy in bringing about revolution.

Typical questions are:

1. 'Was the French Revolution a revolution of all classes of society against the old system of government?'

Write down the names of the classes. Then divide each class into different groups (e.g. divide nobles into courtiers, *noblesse de robe* and provincial nobility). Did they all have the same interests as one another? Make lists of those who supported and those who opposed the 'old system of government'. Why did they do so?

2. 'The French Revolution sprang more from defects in political leadership than from economic distress.' Discuss.

'Political' refers to government and policy-making, so 'political leadership' means that of the King and his ministers. Make a list of all the mistakes made by the King and his ministers. Then write down the causes of the 'economic distress'. Which social groups did it effect and how? You then have to decide whether 'economic distress' or 'political leadership' was more important in bringing about revolution. Avoid sitting on the fence and come to a firm conclusion.

3. 'Was it the absolute power of the French monarchy or its weakness that caused the Revolution of 1789?'

For the 'absolute power of the French monarchy' you will have to refer to your notes from Chapter 2. In what sense was the French monarchy absolute? You may decide that it was not absolute and that it was the limitations on its power (e.g. the privileges of the *parlements*) that enabled opposition to make itself heard and to grow. In what sense was the monarchy 'weak' – structurally or because Louis XVI was a feeble king? What did he do which showed he was weak? Did his actions lead to revolution?

Source-based questions on 'The Origins of the French Revolution'

1 The *cahiers*
Study the contents of the *cahiers* on pages 27–8 and then answer the following questions:
a) In what respects are the noble *cahiers* more liberal than those of the Third Estate?
b) What privileges were the nobles prepared to give up?
c) On what did the two Estates agree?

2   The Tennis Court Oath

The painting by David on page 31 is propaganda for the revolutionary cause. Look at it carefully and then answer the following
questions:

a) Why do you think that one of the deputies (on the extreme right
   of the picture, with his hands across his chest) is looking so
   dejected?
b) Why do most of the deputies and onlookers have their arms
   outstretched?
c) What do you think is the significance of the group of three in the
   centre foreground of the picture?
d) What do you think the umbrella turned inside out and the
   curtains blowing into the room symbolise?

3   The August Decrees

Read carefully the selection from the August Decrees on pages 36–37
and Bailly's report on pages 37–8. Answer the following questions:

a) Is it true that the National Assembly 'abolishes the feudal regime
   entirely'?
b) What did the peasants gain from the August Decrees?
c) In what respects would they have felt dissatisfied with them?
d) What other changes did the August Decrees bring about? How
   important were they?

CHAPTER 4

The Revolution and the Monarchy, 1789–92

1 The Revolution Consolidated

The August Decrees cleared the ground for the erection of a constitution, but first of all the deputies decided to lay down the principles on which it should be based. The Declaration of the Rights of Man and the Citizen in August 1789 condemned the practices of the *ancien régime* and expressed the broad agreement which was to be found in the *cahiers* of all three orders. It stated that:

1. Men are born free and equal in their rights.
2. The aim of every political association is the maintenance of the natural and imprescriptible rights of man. Those rights are those of liberty, property, security and resistance to oppression.
3. The fundamental source of all sovereignty resides in the nation.
4. Liberty consists in being able to do anything which does not harm another.
7. No man may be accused, arrested or detained except in cases determined by the law.
10. No one must be troubled on account of his opinions, even his religious beliefs, provided that their expression does not disturb public order under the law.
11. Free expression of thought and opinions is one of the most precious rights of man. Accordingly every citizen may speak, write and publish freely.
13. General taxation is indispensable for the upkeep of the public force and for the expenses of government. It should be borne equally by all the citizens in proportion to their means.
14. Every citizen has the right, in person or through his representative, to establish the necessity for a tax, freely to consent to it.
17. . . . the right to property is inviolable and sacred.

The Declaration was to long outlast the constitution to which it was later attached and was to be an inspiration to liberals throughout Europe in the nineteenth century (see Chapter 7).

The King did not share the general enthusiasm for the changes that were taking place and on 5 August he wrote to the Archbishop of Arles:

'I will never consent to the spoliation of my clergy and of my nobility. I will not sanction decrees by which they are despoiled'. He could not use force against the Assembly as the army was unreliable, so he adopted a policy of non-cooperation and refused to promulgate the August Decrees and the Declaration of Rights. This forced the Assembly to consider the important question of what rights the King should have. Should he be able to veto or delay legislation passed by the Assembly? The deputies decided that the King should have a suspensive veto and be able to delay for up to four years laws passed by the Assembly.

There was the further question of whether there should be a single Chamber for the Assembly, or two, as in England and America. Many thought that a second Chamber would be a means by which the aristocracy could recover some of the power they had lost, so the Assembly voted overwhelmingly against this in September. No-one considered abolishing the monarchy completely and setting up a republic. It was decided that the legislative power resided in the National Assembly and that no taxes or loans could be raised without its consent but that 'The supreme executive power resides exclusively in the King's hands . . . The King's person is inviolable and sacred.'

The King refused to approve the Assembly's decrees, but was forced to do so by another revolutionary *journée*. This was prompted by a banquet, held by the King's Guards at Versailles on 1 October to celebrate the arrival of the Flanders regiment, during which there were anti-revolutionary demonstrations. Officers trampled on the tricolour cockade and replaced it with the white cockade of the Bourbons. When news of this reached Paris feelings ran high and there were demands that the King should be brought back to the capital.

This demand coincided with a food shortage in Paris. On 5 October a crowd of women stormed the *Hôtel de Ville*, the headquarters of the Commune, demanding bread. They were persuaded to march to Versailles to put their complaints to the King and the Assembly. Six or seven thousand of them set off on the five hour march. Later in the day 20 000 National Guards, under Lafayette, followed them. When the women reached Versailles they invaded the Assembly and sent a deputation to the King, who agreed to provide Paris with grain. He also agreed to approve the August Decrees and the Declaration of Rights. On 6 October at the request of the crowd, the King and Queen appeared on a balcony and were greeted with cries of 'To Paris'. That afternoon the royal family left Versailles for the Tuileries.

*The 'October Days' were a turning-point in the Revolution. Once in Paris the King regarded himself as a prisoner of the Paris mob and therefore not bound by anything he was forced to accept. When Parisians had revolted in July they had seen the Assembly as their ally. In October the Assembly had been ignored and humiliated. When the deputies followed the King to Paris, some of them felt as much imprisoned as the King did. Most deputies wanted to work out a compromise with Louis, but this was much more difficult for them in Paris, surrounded by a population which could impose its will on the Assembly by another *journée*. Mercy Argentau, the Austrian ambassador, realised this soon after the fall of the Bastille, when he wrote:

1 However unbelievable the Revolution that has just been accomplished may appear, it is none the less absolutely certain that from now on the city of Paris has assumed the role of a king in France and that it can, if it pleases, send an army of forty to fifty
5 thousand citizens to surround the Assembly and dictate laws to it.

From now on the moderate majority of deputies distrusted the population of Paris as much as they did the King, although it was the popular *journées* which had enabled them to defeat Louis in the first place.

2 The Reforms of the Constituent Assembly

After October 1789 most Frenchmen believed that the Revolution was over. For the next year there was broad agreement amongst the different groups in the Assembly, as they set about reorganising French government, laws, finances and the economy. In doing this they tried to apply the principles of the Declaration of Rights and give France a uniform, decentralised, representative and humanitarian system. The deputies regarded themselves as heirs of the Enlightenment and sought to end conflict, cruelty, superstition and poverty. Though nearly everyone wanted to retain a limited monarchy, there were few regrets about the passing of the *ancien régime*. 'People were so weary of the Court,' wrote Ferrières, a noble deputy, 'that most of the nobles were what was subsequently known as democrats'. France was fundamentally changed in many ways. New institutions and attitudes took root that have survived until the present day.

a) Local Government

In restructuring local government the deputies wanted to make sure that power was decentralised, passing from the central government in Paris to the local authorities. This would make it much more difficult for the King to recover the power he had held before the Revolution. They also wanted to ensure that all officials would be elected and would be responsible to those who elected them.

By decrees of December 1789 and January 1790 France was divided into 83 departments (see map on page 60), which were subdivided into 547 districts and 43 360 communes (or municipalities). Communes were grouped into cantons, whose only purpose was to act as areas where primary assemblies for elections were held and justices of the peace had their courts. All these administrative divisions, except the cantons, were run by elected councils. All 'active' citizens, who paid the equivalent of three days' labour in taxes, voted for the municipal officials. Citizens who did not pay this amount in taxes had no vote and were known as 'passive' citizens. 'Active' citizens also voted in the primary assemblies when national elections were held. They could not, however, become officials unless they paid the equivalent of ten days' labour in taxes. This second tier of 'active' citizens elected members of the district and department assemblies and could become officials there. They elected the deputies to the National Assembly too. There was yet another tier of 'active' citizens – to become a deputy in the National Assembly an 'active' citizen had to pay a *marc d' argent* (equivalent to 50 days' labour) in direct taxation. The electoral system was, therefore, heavily weighted in favour of the wealthy, although 61 per cent of Frenchmen had the right to take part in some elections (in England only 4 per cent of adult males had the vote). At municipal level most peasants had the right to vote and were qualified to stand for office. This amounted to an administrative revolution. Before 1789 government officials ran the provincial administration: there was not one elected council. In 1790 there were no government officials at the local level: elected councils had replaced them.

Who controlled these councils? In the south bourgeois landowners controlled them. In the north the bourgeoisie was largely urban and took office in the towns, which left the rural communes in the hands of *laboureurs*, small merchants and artisans. Social groups who had never held any public office now had the opportunity of doing so. It is estimated that in the decade 1789–99 about a million people were elected to councils and gained experience in local administration. These councils had an enormous burden of work thrust upon them in December 1789 – much more than the *cahiers* had asked for. They had to assess and collect direct taxes, maintain law and order, carry out public works, see to the upkeep of churches and control the National Guard. Later legislation added to their responsibilities: they had to administer the clerical oath of loyalty; register births, marriages and deaths; requisition grain and keep a watch on people suspected of opposing the Revolution.

How effective were the councils in carrying out their many duties? In the towns there was usually an adequate supply of literate, talented people, who provided a competent administration. In the villages it was often impossible to fill the councils with men who could read and write. Rural communes, therefore, often carried out their duties badly. In strongly Catholic areas officials disliked persecuting priests who had refused to take the oath of loyalty. Consequently, many resigned and areas were left without any effective local government.

b) Finance

After the royal administration collapsed in 1789 few taxes were collected. The Assembly needed money quickly, particularly when it decided that venal office-holders should be compensated for the loss of their offices. Yet a new tax system could not be set up immediately. It decided, therefore, that the existing system of direct and indirect taxation should continue until 1791. This was very unpopular. People wanted the demands made in the *cahiers* to be carried out at once. When there were outbreaks of violence in Picardy, one of the most heavily taxed areas under the *ancien régime*, the government gave way. The *gabelle* was abolished in March 1790 and within a year nearly all the unpopular indirect taxes, except for external customs duties, were also abolished.

To provide money for the state in the period before the new system operated effectively, the Assembly voted in November 1789 that church property was 'at the disposal of the nation'. Church lands would be sold for the benefit of the state, which would then be responsible for paying the clergy, as the Church would lose most of its income (it had already lost the tithe). The sale was seen as guaranteeing the success of the Revolution: those who bought church lands would have a vested interest in maintaining it, as a restoration of the *ancien régime* might lead to the Church recovering its land. It was also hoped that the clergy would support the new regime, as they would be dependent on it for their salaries. The government would issue bonds, soon known as *assignats*, which the public would buy and use for the purchase of church lands. In April 1790 the Assembly converted the bonds into paper money, like bank notes, which could be used in all financial transactions.

Who bought the church lands or *biens nationaux* ('national properties'), as they were known? The main beneficiaries were the bourgeoisie, as they had the ready cash available and the *biens* were sold off in large lots. They bought most of the lands near the towns. Peasants fared better away from the towns. Lefebvre made a special study of the Nord department and found that by 1799 25 per cent of the land there had been sold as *biens nationaux*: of this peasants had bought 52 per cent, bourgeoisie 48 per cent. About a third of the peasants were first-time owners, so land did not go only to the wealthier *laboureurs*. Even where the bourgeoisie bought most of the land, they often resold it piecemeal to the peasants, especially in the east. It is estimated that the number of peasant smallholders increased by a million between 1789 and 1810.

The new financial system began in January, 1791. As indirect taxes were abolished, the main tax was one on land, to replace the *taille* and the *vingtième*. This was like the tax proposed by Calonne in 1787 and was expected to bring in 75 per cent of total receipts. Twenty per cent was to come from a property tax, which people complained was the old *capitation* in a new form, and the rest from customs duties. Municipal councils were to collect the taxes. This system might have worked well if there had been a systematic valuation of the land, but for this a large number of officials was needed. The Assembly would not provide them, as they would cost too much. Consequently, a survey of land values was not begun until 1807 and was not completed until the 1830s. Meanwhile, the new tax rolls were based on those of the *ancien régime*, so that great regional variations remained. People in the Seine et Marne department, for example, paid five times as much in taxes as those in the Arriège.

Was the new system better than the old? The poor certainly benefited, as the burden of taxation fell on producers rather than consumers, with the abolition of indirect taxes. It was a fairer system, as all property and income was to be taxed on the same basis. The new financial structure was to last in its essentials throughout the nineteenth century.

c) Economic Reforms

All the deputies in the Constituent Assembly believed in *laissez-faire*: that trade and industry should be free from any government interference. They therefore introduced free trade in grain in August 1789 and removed price controls. These measures were extended to other products from 1790–1, though this is not what the people as a whole desired. They wanted the price and distribution of all essential goods to be controlled, so as to avoid scarcity, high prices and possible starvation. In October 1790 internal tariffs were abolished, so a national market was created for the first time. This was helped by the creation of a single system of weights and measures – the decimal system – which applied to the whole of France.

The deputies were determined to get rid of any corporations which had special privileges. Guilds were therefore abolished in 1791, as they restricted the entry of people into certain trades. In June 1791 a coalition of 80 000 Parisian workers was threatening a general strike to obtain higher wages, so the Assembly passed the Le Chapelier law, named after the deputy who proposed it, which forbade trade unions and employers' organisations. Collective bargaining, picketing and strikes were declared illegal. This has been described as 'class' legislation, as it was passed in response to the petitions of manufacturers and harmed the interests of the workers. No one in the Assembly objected. Strikes remained illegal until 1864: the ban on trade unions was not lifted until 1884.

The Assembly regarded relief for the poor as a duty of the state. The Church had provided what little assistance the poor had received but it could do so no longer when it lost its main sources of income. There was, therefore, an urgent need for a national organisation, financed by taxation, to take over this role. The Assembly set up a committee which, in 1791, showed for the first time just how serious the problem was: it concluded that nearly two million people could support themselves only by begging. When it came to taking practical measures to help the poor the committee found itself impotent: there was simply not enough money available to deal with such an appalling problem, so nothing was done.

d) Justice

The Constituent Assembly applied the same principle of uniformity to the legal system as it had done to local government. Instead of different systems of law in the north and south and different types of lawcourt, there were to be the same law and law-courts throughout France. *Lettres de cachet* had already been made illegal by the Declaration of Rights. Between 1789 and 1792 all the old law courts – the *parlements*, seigneurial and ecclesiastical courts – were swept away and replaced by a new, uniform system, which was based on the administrative divisions of the reformed local government. In each canton there was to be a justice of the peace, who handled many cases which had previously gone to the seigneurial courts. His main task was to persuade the different parties to come to an agreement but he could also judge minor civil cases without appeal. More serious civil cases went to the district court. There was to be a criminal court in each department, where trials would be held in public and a jury of twelve citizens, chosen by ballot, would decide on questions of guilt or innocence. The idea of having a jury, like that of having justices of the peace, was taken from English law. At the head of the judicial system was a Court of Appeal, whose judges were elected by the department assemblies. All judges were elected by active citizens but only those who had been lawyers for five years could be elected. This ensured that all judges were well qualified and accountable.

There were other changes too which improved the quality of French justice. The penal code was made more humane: torture and mutilation were abolished. Anyone arrested had to be brought before a court within 24 hours. The number of crimes for which death was the penalty was vastly reduced and from March 1792 the same speedy method of execution (the guillotine) was to be used for all condemned to death.

The new judicial system was one of the most lasting reforms of the Constituent Assembly. For the first time, justice became accessible, impartial and cheap and was therefore popular. The French system of justice had been one of the most backward, barbarous and corrupt in Europe. In two years it became one of the most enlightened.

e) Religion

The Constituent Assembly wanted to create a church that was free from abuses, free from foreign (papal) control, democratic and linked to the new system of local government. The deputies were not anti-religious or anti-Catholic. They simply wanted to extend to religion the principles they applied elsewhere. They also wanted to tie the Catholic Church in France more closely to the state than it had been under the *ancien régime*, as this would strengthen the Revolution. They had certainly no intention of interfering with the doctrines of the Church or with its spiritual functions.

In August 1789 the Assembly abolished the tithe, annates (payments by Catholics to the Pope) and pluralism (the holding of more than one clerical office, such as a bishopric). It also ended the old corporate privileges of the Church, such as its right to decide how much taxation it would pay. Most clergy supported these measures. They also accepted the sale of church lands, because they would be paid more than they had been under the *ancien régime*. In February 1790 a decree distinguished between monastic orders which did not work in the community and those which provided education and charity. The former were suppressed, as they made no direct contribution to the common good. The latter were allowed to remain 'for the present', although the taking of religious vows was forbidden. These changes took place without creating much of a stir among the clergy as a whole. Less popular was the decree in December 1789 giving civil rights to Protestants. These rights were extended to Jews in September 1791.

There was no serious conflict with the Church until the Civil Constitution of the Clergy in July 1790. This adapted the organisation of the Church to the administrative framework of local government. Dioceses were to coincide with departments. This meant that the number of bishoprics would be reduced from 135 to 83. There would not only be fewer bishops but fewer clergy generally, as all clerical posts except for parish priests and bishops ceased to exist. The attempt to extend democracy to all aspects of government was also applied to the Church. Clergy were no longer to be appointed but were to be elected: bishops by departmental electors, *curés* by those in the districts. A link with the Pope was cut as he lost the right to confirm new bishops. All clergy had to reside in their diocese or parish. But there was no intention of ending the Catholic Church's position as the State Church in France.

Most clergy opposed the principle of election but, even so, the majority (including many bishops) were in favour of finding a way of accepting the Civil Constitution. They demanded that the reforms be submitted to a national synod of the French Church. This would have made a compromise possible but the Constituent Assembly would not agree to this, as it believed that it would make the Church a privileged corporation in the state once again and a separate order, something which had just been abolished. As a church assembly was not allowed to discuss the matter, the clergy waited for the Pope to give his verdict. He delayed coming to a decision, as he was involved in delicate negotiations with the French over the status of Avignon, papal territory inside France. The Assembly grew tired of waiting and in November 1790 decreed that clergy must take an oath to the Constitution. This split the clergy. In the Assembly only two of the 44 bishops and a third of the other clergy took the oath. In France as a whole seven bishops and 55 per cent of the clergy took the oath. When the Pope finally condemned the Civil Constitution in March and April 1791, many clergy who had taken the oath retracted.

    *The Civil Constitution of the Clergy had momentous results. Deputies in the Assembly were shocked when it was rejected by many clergy and by the Pope. There were now in effect two Catholic Churches in France. One, the constitutional Church, accepted the Revolution and was rejected by Rome. The other, a non-juring Church (those who refused to take the oath were known as 'non-jurors' or 'refractories'), was approved by the Pope but regarded by patriots as against the Revolution. One major effect of this split was that the counter-revolution, the movement which sought to overturn the Revolution, received mass support for the first time. Before it had been supported only by a few royalists and *émigrés*. In the most strongly Catholic areas – the west, north-east and south of the Massif Central – few clergy took the oath. Many villagers complained that the Assembly was trying to change their religion, especially when refractory priests were expelled. They felt a sense of betrayal which, combined with their hostility to other measures of the Assembly, such as conscription, was to lead to open revolt in 1793 in areas such as the Vendée (see page 72). Disaffection with the Revolution, which eventually turned into civil war, was, therefore, one result of the Civil Constitution of the Clergy. Another result was the King's attempt to flee from France in June 1791 (see page 53), precipitating a series of events which was to bring about the downfall of the monarchy.

3   The Revolutionary Clubs and Popular Discontent

Political clubs had begun to form soon after the Estates-General met in May 1789. The Jacobin Club originated in meetings of radical Breton deputies with others of similar views. When the Assembly moved to Paris after the October Days it met in premises rented from the Dominicans, who were nicknamed Jacobins. There its members debated measures that were to come before the Assembly. As it had a high entrance fee, its members – there were 1200 by July 1790 – came mainly from the wealthiest sections of society. The dominant members of the Jacobin Club up to the summer of 1791 were liberal constitutional monarchists. Robespierre was the leader of a minority group of radical Jacobin deputies. A national network of Jacobin clubs soon grew up. There were 900 such clubs by the spring of 1791.

The Cordeliers Club, founded in April 1790, was more radical than the Jacobin Club and had unrestricted admission. It objected to the distinction between 'active' and 'passive' citizens and supported measures which the *sans-culottes* favoured: direct democracy, the recall of deputies to account for their actions and the right of insurrection. It had much support among the working-class, although its leaders were bourgeois. Danton and Desmoulins were lawyers. Hébert was an unsuccessful writer who had become a journalist when freedom of the press was allowed. Brissot was also a journalist, but the most notorious writer of all was Marat, a failed doctor. He hated all those who had enjoyed privileges under the old regime and attacked them violently in his newspaper, *L'Ami du Peuple*. He became the chief spokesman of the popular movement.

During the winter of 1790–1 the example of the Cordeliers Club led to the formation of many 'popular' or 'fraternal' societies, which were soon to be found in every district in Paris and in several provincial towns. In 1791 the Cordeliers Club and the popular societies formed a federation and elected a central committee. The members of the popular societies were drawn mainly from the liberal professions, officials, skilled artisans and shopkeepers. Labourers rarely joined, as they did not have the spare time for politics.

As there were no political parties, the clubs played an important part in the Revolution. They kept the public informed of the major issues of the day, supported election candidates and acted as pressure groups to influence deputies in the Assembly and to promote actions which the deputies seemed reluctant to undertake.

*Peasants and *sans-culottes* were not satisfied with what they had received from the Revolution. When the peasants realised in the spring of 1790 that their harvest dues were not abolished outright but would have to be bought out, they were deeply disillusioned. A rural revolution began in 1790 in Brittany, central France and the south-east, which lasted until 1792. Peasants fixed the price of grain, called for the sale of *biens* in small lots and attacked *châteaux*. The rising in the Midi (Languedoc, Provence and the Rhône valley) in 1792 was as important as any in 1789 in size and the extent of the destruction.

The *sans-culottes* (so-called because they wore trousers rather than the knee-breeches of the upper classes) were the workers in the towns. They were not a class, as they included artisans and master craftsmen, who owned their own workshops, as well as wage-earners. They had been responsible for the successful attack on the Bastille and for bringing the royal family back to Paris in the October Days, yet they had received few rewards. Many of them were 'passive' citizens, who did not have the vote. They suffered greatly from inflation. To meet its expenses the government printed more and more *assignats*, whose value declined. There was a wave of strikes by workers against the falling value of their wages early in 1791. Grain prices rose by up to 50 per cent after a poor harvest in 1791. This resulted in riots, when crowds forced shopkeepers to reduce prices. The discontent of the workers could be used by the popular societies, who linked economic protests to the political demand for a democratic republic, and by groups in the Assembly who were seeking power. This made the Revolution more radical in ways which the bourgeois leaders of 1789 had neither intended nor desired.

4 The Rise of a Republican Movement

a) The Flight to Varennes

Mirabeau was the outstanding politician and orator in the Constituent Assembly. He had been a member of the Committee of Thirty and, although he was a noble, had been elected to represent the Third Estate in the Estates-General. He was a monarchist but saw that the monarchy would have to change if it was to survive. He wanted a limited monarchy, with the government responsible to the Assembly. He alone could have provided effective leadership but he failed to do so because he was not trusted. From May 1790 he was closely associated with the Court, which settled his debts and paid him a pension. In return, he advised the King by correspondence and defended royal interests as best he could in the Assembly. This was regarded as treachery by the other deputies, as they suspected that the King wished to restore royal despotism.

When Mirabeau died in April 1791 the moderates were becoming more influential in the Assembly. They feared the new clubs and the emergence of an organised working-class movement. They wanted to end the Revolution but for this to happen there had to be a compromise with the King. This was difficult, as anyone suspected of negotiating with the King would be accused of selling out to the Court. There was also no means of knowing if the King was sincerely prepared to co-operate with the moderates. Louis dashed all their hopes by attempting to flee.

Louis XVI was a devout man, who deeply regretted his acceptance of the Civil Constitution of the Clergy, which offended his conscience. He decided to flee to Montmédy in Lorraine, on the border of Luxembourg, and put himself under the protection of the military commander of the area. There he could renegotiate with the Constituent Assembly the parts of the Constitution he disliked, from a position of strength. Military action would, it was hoped, be unnecessary, although the King was aware that there was a danger that his flight might bring about civil war.

Louis left Paris with his family on 20 June 1791. When he reached Varennes, 30 miles short of his goal, he was recognised and stopped. He was brought back to Paris amidst an icy silence. Louis' younger brother, the Comte de Provence, was luckier than the King. He too fled from Paris on 20 June with his wife but he arrived safely in Brussels the next day.

One immediate result of the flight was that the King lost what remained of his popularity, which had depended on his being seen to support the Revolution. Royal inn signs and street names disappeared all over Paris. His flight persuaded many who had hitherto supported him that he could no longer be trusted. People started to talk openly of replacing the monarchy by a republic. The deputies in the Assembly acted calmly in this situation. They did not want a republic. They feared that the declaration of a republic would lead to civil war in France and war with European monarchs. Nor did they want to concede victory to the radicals, who wanted more democratic policies. 'Are we going to end the Revolution or are we going to start it again?' one deputy asked the Assembly. On 16 July the Assembly voted to suspend the King until the constitution was completed. He would be restored only after he had sworn to observe it. This was going too far for some deputies – 290 abstained from voting in future as a protest. For others, suspension did not go far enough.

b) The Champ de Mars

The radicals were appalled when the King was not dethroned or put on trial. Their anger was directed against the Assembly, which they claimed no longer represented the people. The Cordeliers took the lead with the popular societies and persuaded the Jacobins to join them in supporting a petition for the King's deposition. This split the Jacobin Club. Those who did not want the King deposed – and this included nearly all the deputies who were members – left the Club. Robespierre was left to preside over the more radical rump. It seemed as though the Jacobins had destroyed themselves but only 72 of the Jacobin clubs in France defected and most of these drifted back in the next few months. Meanwhile the Parisian defectors formed a new club, the Feuillants, which, for the moment, had control of the Assembly.

On 17 July 1791, 50 000 people flocked to the Champ de Mars, a huge field where the Feast of the Federation, celebrating the fall of the Bastille, had been held three days earlier. They were there to sign a republican petition on the 'altar of the fatherland'. This was a political demonstration of the poorer sections of the Paris population. The Commune, under pressure from the Assembly, declared martial law. They sent Lafayette with the National Guard to the Champ de Mars, where the Guard fired on the peaceful and unarmed crowd. About 50 people were killed.

This was the first bloody clash between different groups in the Third Estate, and it was greeted with pleasure in the Assembly. Messages of support for the Assembly poured in from the provinces. Martial law remained in force for a month, during which time some popular leaders were arrested. Others, such as Hébert, Marat and Danton fled or went into hiding. The moderates had won – it took nearly a year for the popular movement to recover – and could now work out a compromise with the King without facing mob violence.

The Feuillants were now more than ever committed to making an agreement with the King. They did not trust him but they had lost popular support. They controlled Paris and the Assembly for the moment but their long-term success depended on the cooperation of Louis, which was far from certain.

c) The Constitution of 1791

One of the main aims of the Constituent Assembly had been to draw up a constitution, which would replace an absolute monarchy by a limited one. Real power was to pass to an elected assembly. Much of the Constitution – that the King should have a suspensive veto and that there should be one elected assembly – had been worked out in 1789 but the rest was not finally passed until September 1791. The King had the right to appoint his ministers (although they could not be members of the Assembly) and military commanders. His suspensive veto could not be applied to financial or constitutional matters. He was dependent on the Assembly for his foreign policy, as he needed its consent before he could declare war. The King, whose office was hereditary, was subordinate to the Assembly, as it passed the laws which the King had to obey. 'In France there is no authority superior to the law . . . it is only by means of the law that the King reigns'. In September the King was forced, reluctantly, to accept the Constitution. Marie Antoinette's attitude was that it was 'so monstrous that it cannot survive for long'. She was determined to overthrow it at the first opportunity.

d) The Legislative Assembly

When the King accepted the Constitution in September 1791, the Constituent Assembly was dissolved. By this time suspicion and hatred amongst the deputies had replaced the euphoria of 1789. This change had come about because of the King's reluctance to accept measures he disliked and because of the fear of counter-revolutionary plots. To prevent his opponents from dominating the next Assembly, Robespierre proposed a self-denying ordinance, which was passed, that no member of the Constituent Assembly could sit in the next Legislative Assembly.

In the ensuing elections under a quarter of the 'active' citizens voted.

They elected an Assembly which was almost wholly bourgeois. There were few nobles, most of whom retired to their estates and kept a low profile, hoping for better times. Only 23 clergy were elected; there were no peasants or artisans and few businessmen. At the beginning 264 deputies were members of the Feuillant Club, who considered the Revolution to be over, and 136 deputies were members of the Jacobin Club. About 350 deputies did not belong either to the Feuillants or the Jacobins.

The deputies were worried by the non-juring clergy and by the *émigrés*, whose numbers had increased greatly since the flight to Varennes. Nearly all the *ancien régime* bishops and many of the great court and *parlementaire* families had emigrated. What alarmed the Assembly most was the desertion of army officers. By early 1791, 1200 noble officers had joined the *émigrés*, though a large majority of pre-Revolution officers remained at their posts. All this changed after Varennes. By the end of 1791 about 6000 had emigrated, 60 per cent of all officers. The Assembly, therefore, passed two laws in November. One declared that all non-jurors were suspects. The other said that all *émigrés* who did not return to France by 1 January 1792 would forfeit their property and be regarded as traitors. When the King vetoed these laws his unpopularity increased: he appeared to be undermining the Revolution.

Yet in spite of the mistrust of the King, it seemed likely that the Constitution of 1791 would survive. What prevented this was the war with Austria, which began in April 1792. This event had more decisive and far-reaching results than any other in the whole of the Revolution. Almost everything that happened in France from that time was caused, or affected, by it. The war finally destroyed the consensus of 1789. It led directly to the fall of the monarchy, to civil war and to the Terror.

e) The Coming of War

The Great Powers had shown no interest in intervening during the first two years of the French Revolution. Leopold II, the Habsburg Emperor, approved of many of the liberal reforms in the Revolution and did not want a return to absolutism in France. He, like other sovereigns, was pleased at the collapse of French power and no longer regarded France as a serious rival. In any case, Russia, Austria and Prussia were occupied elsewhere. From 1787 Russia and Austria were at war with the Ottoman Empire. Leopold abandoned the fight in July 1790 to concentrate on the Austrian Netherlands (Belgium), where there was a revolt. He crushed this in the winter of 1790 and then turned his attention to Poland, where Russia and Prussia were seeking to gain territory. All three powers were more interested in what was happening in Poland than in what was going on in France.

After the flight to Varennes the Austrians felt they had to make some gesture in support of Louis. Therefore, in August 1791, they issued the Declaration of Pillnitz in association with Prussia. This said that they were ready with the other sovereigns of Europe to restore the King of France to a position from which he could strengthen the foundations of monarchical government. This appeared to be a threat to interfere in French internal affairs but in reality it was no threat at all. The Austrians knew that the other powers, such as Britain, would not join them, so the Declaration would not lead to any action. In France the Declaration did not create much of a stir. The Assembly did not debate it and most newspapers ignored it. When the Constitution was passed in September, Leopold gave it a warm welcome, so the possibility of Austrian intervention was even more remote.

In France, meanwhile, there were several people who, for very different reasons, came to believe that war was in their own best interests or those of France. Marie Antoinette ('the only man in the family', Mirabeau called her) wrote to her brother Leopold in September 1791: 'Conciliation is out of the question now. Armed force has destroyed everything and only armed force can put things right'. She hoped for a war in which France would be defeated, enabling Louis to recover his old powers. The King shared her view that France would be defeated. 'The physical condition and morale of France', he wrote, 'is such that it will be unable to sustain even half a campaign.' At the same time as he was taking an oath to defend the Constitution, the Queen was writing to the Austrian ambassador: 'giving the impression of adopting the new ideas is the safest way of quickly defeating them'. The deputies were not taken in. Rumours abounded that the country's foreign policy was being run by an 'Austrian Committee', headed by Marie Antoinette, and that secret agents were being sent to Koblenz (the headquarters of the *émigrés*) and Vienna to plot counter-revolution. These rumours were well founded.

Army commanders like Lafayette and Dumouriez also wanted war. Lafayette, the first commander of the National Guard, had brought the King from Versailles to Paris in the October Days and was responsible for the 'massacre' of the Champ de Mars. He had become disillusioned by the failure of the Revolution to produce political stability and wanted the authority of the King to be strengthened. This could be done by waging a short, successful war against Austria, which would also increase his prestige as a general. It would enable him to dictate his own terms to both the King and the Assembly.

The desire for war resulted in the cooperation of Lafayette and his followers with the Brissotins, who also wanted war. The Brissotins were not a party but a group of deputies who took their name from their leader, Jacques Brissot. They merged with some deputies from the Gironde department in south-western France and so were also known as Girondins. Brissot was one of the first to support a republic and after the flight from Varennes wanted the abolition of the monarchy and the trial of Louis XVI. He saw that the King had not really accepted the Constitution and that the Court was intriguing against the Revolution and seeking the armed intervention of the European powers. A war would force the King to come out into the open, as it would expose traitors and those who were opposed to the Revolution.

There were about 130 Girondins in the Assembly, so to obtain a majority they needed the support of Lafayette and his followers and of the unorganised centre. This Brissot obtained by playing on their hopes and fears in a campaign for war which began in October 1791. He maintained that a successful war would rouse enthusiasm for the Revolution and show the permanence of the new regime. In a war the appeal of revolutionary ideals abroad would be irresistible and French armies would have the active support of the enemy's own repressed subjects. Brissot thought that the international situation was promising for France. The European powers would not unite against France because Britain would not join in, Russia was preoccupied with Poland and Prussia was more likely to fight for France than against her.

Most deputies were won over by these arguments but some politicians outside the Assembly, particularly Robespierre, were not. He was not a member of the Assembly because of the self-denying ordinance, so he made known his impassioned opposition to war in the Jacobin Club. Open opponents of the Revolution, he said, were too discredited to be a danger unless they could shelter behind constitutional monarchists. The real threat, therefore, came from soldiers like Lafayette, who were still popular enough to mislead the public. They were secret agents of the Court and so war would be 'merely a means of overthrowing the Constitution, merely the final stage of a deep plot to destroy liberty'. 'You propose to give supreme power to those who most want your ruin', he said. 'The only way to save the state and to safeguard freedom is to wage war in the right way, on our enemies at home, instead of marching under their orders against their allies across the frontiers.' The only people to benefit from the war would be generals, speculators, the Court and noble conspirators. He saw that the European powers aimed at intimidating France, not invading her. War would be more difficult than Brissot expected, because foreigners would not rise up in support of French invaders: 'no one loves armed missionaries.' Robespierre became isolated and unpopular and convinced that those who accused him of a lack of patriotism were conniving with the Court and deliberately betraying the Revolution. His relations with Brissot were poisoned by bitter personal quarrels and the suspicion of each other's motives which underlay them.

The Girondins were pressing hard for war but it is doubtful whether they would have gained the support of the majority of deputies without the bungling of Austria and Prussia. On 7 February 1792 Prussia and Austria became allies and thought they could intimidate the French by threatening war. They had great confidence in their own armies: in

1789 a small Prussian army had conquered the United Provinces in under a month. In 1790 a small Austrian army occupied Belgium in under two weeks. They believed France to be weak from civil war and mutinies in the army as well as bankrupt. She would have neither the will nor the ability to resist Austrian pressure.

* Austrian threats and Girondin attacks on the 'Austrian Committee' at Court forced the King to dismiss his Feuillant ministers in March 1792 and appoint a more radical government, including some Girondin ministers. This was a decisive change. The old ministers had carried out the wishes of the King: the new ones obeyed the Assembly. Both the Assembly and the government now wanted war, especially the new Foreign Minister, General Dumouriez. He hated Austria but had aims similar to those of Lafayette: a short successful war would increase his own personal power and that of the Crown. In Austria the pacific Leopold had died on 1 March and had been replaced by the young and impetuous Francis II. Austria decided, reluctantly, on war when there were rumours that Marie Antoinette was to be put on trial. But it was the French who actually declared war, on 20 April 1792. Only seven deputies voted against it. The French hoped to fight solely against Austria but Prussia declared war on France a month later and took the lead in the campaign, with the Duke of Brunswick as commander-in-chief.

5   The Fall of the Monarchy

The war showed the weakness of the French armies. Revolutionary propaganda and the emigration of officers had destroyed the discipline of the regular army, whilst volunteers were neither trained nor equipped to fight. The French advance in the Austrian Netherlands was routed on 29 April. Troops panicked and retreated headlong to Lille, where they murdered their commander. Whole units deserted. By the end of May all three field commanders were advising that peace should be made immediately. Allied armies began to invade France. Treason and traitors were blamed for French defeats and with some justification: Marie Antoinette had sent details of French military plans to the Austrians.

The government also had other problems to cope with, such as opposition from non-juring priests and counter-revolutionaries. The Girondins had to satisfy the popular clamour for action against 'traitors'. On 27 May the Assembly passed a law for the deportation of refractory priests. Another law disbanded the King's Guard and a third set up a camp for 20 000 National Guards (they were known as *fédérés* because their arrival was to coincide with the Feast of the Federation on 14 July) from the provinces. They were to protect Paris from invasion and the government from a *coup* by the generals, especially Lafayette. Louis refused to approve these laws. When Roland, the Girondin

France, 1789–95

Minister of the Interior, protested, Louis dismissed him and other Girondin ministers on 13 June. Dumouriez resigned soon afterwards. On 19 June Louis vetoed the laws on refractory priests and the *fédéré* camp.

People expected a military *coup* when a letter from Lafayette was read out in the Assembly on 18 June. He accused the Jacobins of setting up a state within the state and demanded that the Assembly should end the rule of the clubs. Napoleon Bonaparte, who was in Paris at the time, showed how opinion in France was dividing. He observed:

> 1 M. de Lafayette has written to the National Assembly denounc-
> ing the Jacobins. His letter is very strongly expressed . . . M. de
> Lafayette, the majority of officers in the army, all honest men, the
> ministers and the Parisian administration are on one side; on the
> 5 other are most of the Assembly, the Jacobins and the people.

Leaders of the Sections (Paris had been divided into 48 sections to replace the 60 electoral districts of 1789) responded to these events by holding an armed demonstration on 20 June, the anniversary of the Tennis Court Oath and of the flight to Varennes. Their leaders came from the Cordeliers Club. The Jacobins stayed aloof, as they had done at the time of the Champ de Mars petition. About 8000 demonstrators, many of them National Guards, poured into the Tuileries. One participant described what happened, when he reported to the Jacobin Club:

> 1 I have just come from the Tuileries where, at a window, I saw the
> King wearing a red cap . . . He was sitting on a slightly raised seat
> with three or four National Guards and a few deputies at his side.
> The people had entered this apartment in considerable numbers,
> 5 shouting: 'Down with the veto! Ratify the decrees! Long live the
> nation!'
> The King was wearing the cap of liberty on his head and was
> drinking, from a bottle, to the health of the nation. He was unable
> to make himself heard and several times he rang a little bell to get
> 10 them to listen. When he finally got their attention he told them
> that he was in favour of the Constitution and swore to uphold it.
> The people shouted that it wasn't true, that he had already
> deceived them and would do so again and then they went on:
> 'Bring back the patriot ministers!'

Louis behaved with great dignity. He was not intimidated and his calmness may have saved his life. This *journée* did not achieve its desired end: the King did not withdraw his veto or recall the Girondin ministers. However, it did show very clearly the weakness of the King and the Assembly and the power of the Sections.

*The Assembly soon took steps which recognised the growing importance of the *sans-culottes* but which also increased the likelihood of a rising. On 11 July it declared a state of emergency by issuing a decree '*la patrie en danger*' (the fatherland in danger), which called on every Frenchman to fight. This tilted the balance of power in favour of the democrats. How could you ask a man to fight and not give him a vote? The Sections, whose assemblies were allowed to meet in permanent session, and *fédérés* demanded the admission of 'passive' citizens into the sectional assemblies and National Guard, requests which were granted by the end of the month. Thus the middle class control of 1789 crumbled away and the popular democracy of the *sans-culottes* gained ground.

Tension in Paris was increased by the arrival of *fédérés* from the provinces and by the Brunswick Manifesto. The *fédérés* were militant revolutionaries and republicans, unlike the Paris National Guard, whose officers were conservative or royalist. Their patriotism was expressed in the war song of the Rhine army, composed in Strasbourg by Rouget de Lisle. It acquired its name '*La Marseillaise*' as it was sung by the *fédérés* of Marseille on their march to the capital. In July their total number in Paris was never above 5000 but they were a powerful pressure group in the radical sections, calling for the removal of the King.

The Brunswick Manifesto, issued by the commander-in-chief of the Austro-Prussian armies, was published in Paris on 1 August. It threatened that any National Guards captured fighting would be punished 'as rebels to their King'. Parisians were collectively held responsible for the safety of the royal family. If it was harmed the allies would execute 'an exemplary vengeance . . . by delivering the city of Paris to a military execution'. The Manifesto was intended to help the King but it had the opposite effect. Frenchmen were infuriated and many who had supported the monarchy now turned against it.

As a new insurrection was being prepared by radicals and *fédérés* from the middle of July, the Girondins changed their attitude of opposition to the King and tried to prevent a rising. They warned the King that there was likely to be a far more violent uprising than that of 20 June and that he would, at least, be deposed. They offered to do all they could to prevent such an uprising, if he would recall the ministers dismissed on 13 June. Louis haughtily rejected their offer. Meanwhile, the Jacobin leader Robespierre was cooperating with the central committee of the *fédérés* and on 29 July, in a speech to the Jacobin Club, he put forward his proposals. He abandoned his previous support for the Constitution of 1791 and called for the overthrow of the monarchy. He also wanted a National Convention, elected by universal male suffrage to replace the Legislative Assembly, and a purge of the departmental authorities, many of which were royalist. Some of these ideas had been expressed earlier by the Cordeliers, the Sections and the

Commune but they did not become an agreed basis for revolt until they were put forward by Robespierre. Hitherto he had warned the *fédérés* and the Sections against precipitate action, as this might lead to a backlash in the King's favour. Now he felt the moment had come to strike. Petitions were pouring in from the *fédérés*, the clubs and provinces for the removal of the King. On 3 August Pétion, the Mayor of Paris, went to the Legislative Assembly and demanded, on behalf of 47 out of the 48 Sections, the abolition of the monarchy. Yet the Assembly refused to depose the King and defeated a motion to put Lafayette on trial. This finally persuaded many that a rising was necessary.

*On the night of 9 August *sans-culottes* took over the *Hôtel de Ville*, overthrew the old municipality and set up a revolutionary Commune. Its leaders were men like Hébert, who had taken part in the Cordeliers agitation of the last year and had strong links with the Sections and the *fédérés*. The next morning several thousand National Guard, now open to 'passive citizens', and 2000 *fédérés*, led by those from Marseille, marched on the Tuileries. The palace was defended by 3000 troops, 2000 of whom were National Guards. The others were Swiss mercenaries who were certain to resist. During the morning the King sought refuge in the Assembly to protect his family. The National Guard defending the Tuileries joined the insurgents, who entered the courtyards. They believed the attack was over until the Swiss began to fire. The *Marseillais* replied with grapeshot and it seemed that a violent battle was about to take place. At this point the King ordered his Swiss guards to cease fire. This left them defenceless against the vengeance of the attackers: 600 Swiss were massacred. Of the insurgents, 90 *fédérés* and 300 Parisians (tradesmen, craftsmen, wage-earners) had been killed or wounded. It was the most bloody *journée* of the Revolution.

The rising was as much a rejection of the Assembly as it was of the King. The insurgents invaded the Assembly and forced it to recognise the new revolutionary Commune, which had given the orders for the attack on the palace. The deputies had to hand over the King to the Commune, who imprisoned him in the Temple. They also had to agree to the election, by universal male suffrage, of a National Convention to draw up a new, democratic constitution. The Commune was now in control in Paris, though in the rest of France it was the authority of the Assembly alone that was recognised.

The constitutional monarchists, about two-thirds of the deputies, did not feel safe, so they stayed away from the Assembly and went into hiding. This left the Girondins in charge, the beneficiaries of a revolution they had tried to avoid. The 300 deputies remaining in the Assembly appointed new ministers, including the three who had been dismissed earlier. A surprise appointment was that of Danton. He made his career in the Cordeliers Club and the Paris Sections and now became Minister of Justice to please the *sans-culottes*. In its final six weeks, the

Assembly did all that the Commune wanted. It passed several radical measures, including the deportation of refractory priests. Peasant support was more than ever necessary after 10 August, as many provinces resented this latest attack on the monarchy. The Assembly decreed that redeemable feudal dues were abolished without compensation, unless the *seigneur* could produce the title-deeds. This effectively ended the feudal regime, which peasants had unsuccessfully been trying to do since the August Decrees of 1789. The Assembly also ordered that *émigré* lands should be sold in small lots. The King was suspended: it was left for the Convention to decide whether or not to dethrone him.

The Convention met for the first time on 20 September 1792. On the next day it abolished the monarchy.

Making notes on 'The Revolution and the Monarchy, 1789–1792'

Your notes on this period should help you to understand the nature and significance of the reforms of the Constituent Assembly, why war came about and the reasons for the fall of the monarchy. The following headings and sub-headings should ensure you include all the main points:

1.   The Revolution Consolidated
1.1. The Declaration of Rights
1.2. Drafting a new constitution
1.3. The October Days
2.   The Reforms of the Constituent Assembly
2.1. Local government
2.2. Finance
2.3. Economic reforms
2.4. Justice
2.5. Religion, especially the Civil Constitution of the Clergy. What were its far-reaching results?
3.   Revolutionary Clubs and Popular Discontent
3.1. Jacobins
3.2. Cordeliers
3.3. Popular discontent – peasants and *sans-culottes*
4.   The Rise of the Republican Movement
4.1. The flight to Varennes
4.2. The Champ de Mars massacre
4.3. The Constitution of 1791
4.4. The Legislative Assembly
4.5. War – why did it come about?

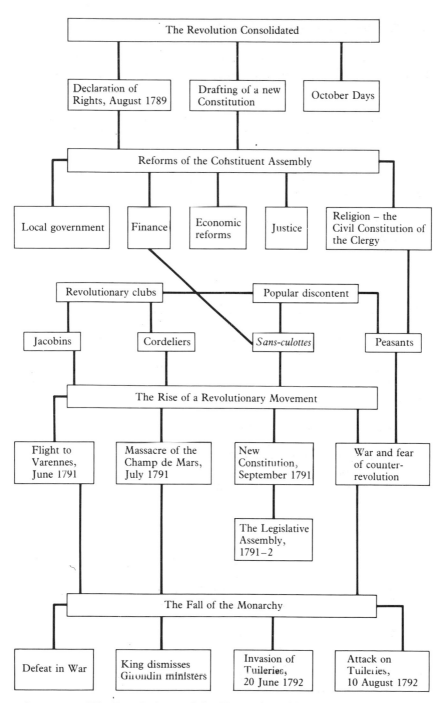

Summary – The Revolution and the Monarchy, 1789–92

5.   The Fall of the Monarchy
5.1.   The war goes badly
5.2.   The King dismisses Girondin ministers
5.3.   Invasion of the Tuileries, 20 June 1792
5.4.   Radicals take control: 'passive' citizens join the National Guard –
       fédérés – the Brunswick Manifesto – a revolutionary Commune
       formed
5.5.   Attack on the Tuileries, 10 August 1792

---

*Answering essay questions on 'The Revolution and the Monarchy,
1789–92'*

You will need some of the information in this chapter to answer general
questions on the period 1789–99. There is a discussion of these
questions on page 131.
    Questions on the period 1789–92 are usually on the Constituent
Assembly or on the fall of the monarchy. Examples are:

1. 'Discuss the importance of the Constituent Assembly in the
   history of the French Revolution.'

In answering a question like this you must first, of course, establish the
dates of the Constituent Assembly (7 July 1789 – 30 September 1791).
Some of the information you need to answer this question will,
therefore, be found in Chapter 3. This question is wider than it appears
to be and will require reference to later chapters, as you have to
compare the significance of what the Constituent Assembly did with
what happened later in the Revolution.

2. 'Why did the attempts to create a limited monarchy in France
   between 1789 and 1792 fail?'

Draw up a list of reasons for (causes of) the fall of the monarchy. These
may include: the character and actions of the King; divisions within the
Assembly; fear of counter-revolution; the actions of revolutionary
clubs; the discontent of the *sans-culottes*; the opening of the National
Guard to 'passive' citizens; the war and initial defeats. When you have
made your list, do not treat all the causes as of equal importance. Try to
produce a hierarchy of causes. Was there one cause, above all others,
which led to the downfall of the monarchy?

Source-based questions on 'The Revolution and the Monarchy, 1789–92'

1 The Declaration of Rights
Read carefully the extracts from the Declaration on page 43 and then answer the following questions:
a) Which practices of the *ancien régime* did the Declaration condemn?
b) How did the Declaration reinforce the August Decrees?
c) In what ways did the Declaration reflect the interests and beliefs of the bourgeoisie?
d) What is meant by 'law is the expression of the general will'?

2 The Declaration of War
Read carefully the views of Marie Antoinette on page 57 and of Robespierre on page 58. Answer the following questions:
a) What did Marie Antoinette mean by 'giving the impression of adopting the new ideas is the safest way of quickly defeating them'?
b) Give in your own words Robespierre's reasons for opposing war.
c) Why did most people take an opposite view from that of Robespierre?

3 The Invasion of The Tuileries, 20 June 1792
Read carefully the comments by Napoleon on page 61 and by a member of the Jacobin Club, also on page 61. Answer the following questions:
a) How does Napoleon betray which side he is on?
b) What is the 'red cap'?
c) Which decrees were the people referring to when they shouted 'Ratify the decrees'?
d) Who were the 'patriotic ministers' and why had they been dismissed?

CHAPTER 5

Revolutionary Government and the Terror

The symbol of the Terror is the guillotine and it is this image which most people have in mind when they think of the French Revolution. Bloodthirsty purges, terrified citizens, dictatorship and the suppression of the liberties which had been so triumphantly announced in the Declaration of Rights of 1789: all are associated with the Terror. Yet the Terror had less influence on the formation of modern France than the great reforms of the Constituent Assembly between 1789 and 1791. The French historians Furet and Richet saw the period from August 1792 to July 1794 as a time when militant *sans-culottes* knocked the Revolution off-course. They forced the country's leaders to adopt policies which were contrary to the liberal reforms of the Constituent Assembly. Their support was necessary to preserve the Revolution but they did not make any permanent gains for themselves or any lasting changes. After the fall of Robespierre, the Revolution, they maintain, returned to its earlier course.

There were two periods of Terror and both are associated with the war abroad. The first began with the attack on the Tuileries on 10 August 1792, included the September Massacres and came to an end with the battle of Valmy, when the allied invasion was held up and then pushed back. The second period began with the *journée* of 31 May – 2 June 1793, when some Girondin deputies were arrested, and ended with the execution of Robespierre and his supporters in July 1794. This second Terror began when French armies were doing badly and France was once again faced with invasion. Its end came shortly after the victory of Fleurus in June 1794, which made the French frontiers secure.

1 The Struggle for Power: Girondins and Jacobins

a) The Convention

All men over 21 could vote in the elections to the Convention, which were held at the end of August and the beginning of September 1792, but the result was distorted by fear and intimidation. In Paris, all who had shown royalist sympathies were disfranchised. Thus all 24 members for Paris were Jacobins, republicans, and supporters of the Commune. Robespierre came head of the poll in the capital. At first there were about 200 Girondins and 100 Jacobins in the Convention. The majority of deputies, uncommitted to either group, were known as the 'Plain' or 'Marsh' because of the middle ground where they sat in the Assembly. About a third of the deputies were lawyers. The proportion representing business and trade had declined to nine per cent (compared with 13 per cent in the Constituent Assembly).

Until 2 June 1793 the history of the Convention is that of a struggle between the Girondins and Jacobins. The latter came to be known as the Montagnards or 'the Mountain' or simply the Left, because they sat on the upper benches of the Assembly to the left of the President's chair. This is a better name for them than Jacobins, as the Girondins too were members of the Jacobin Club, where both groups argued fiercely with one another. Neither group was a party which had an agreed programme or accepted a common discipline. People disapproved of parties, which were regarded as pursuing the selfish interests of the members rather than the common good, very much like the corporations and guilds of the old regime. It is, therefore, very difficult to say how many deputies belonged to each group at any time.

The Girondins and Montagnards were all bourgeois and agreed on most policies. Both strongly believed in the Revolution and the Republic, hated privilege, were anti-clerical and favoured a liberal economic policy. Both wanted a more enlightened and humane France. They differed in the sources of their support and in their deep suspicions of each other. The Girondins had most of the Paris press on their side and had much support in the provinces, though it must be remembered that most Montagnard deputies were also from the provinces. However, the opposition of many Girondins to the *journée* of 10 August lost them the support of the Paris militants. The Montagnards, weaker in the provinces than the Girondins, had the solid backing of the clubs and Sections in Paris. They emerged, therefore, as the main champions of Paris as the centre of the Revolution. The Girondins, on the other hand, supported federalism: the right of the provinces to run their own affairs without interference from Paris. This was very similar to the policy of the Constituent Assembly from 1789–1791. Both Girondins and Montagnards were committed to winning the war but the latter were more flexible in their approach. They realised that the support of the people was needed for military victory and that therefore some of their demands would have to be met. The Girondins thought that Robespierre wanted a bloody dictatorship: the Montagnards were convinced that the Girondins would compromise with conservative, even royalist, forces to stay in power. They, therefore, accused them of supporting counter-revolution.

As neither side had a majority in the Assembly each needed to have the support of the Plain. They too were bourgeois, believed in economic liberalism and were deeply afraid of the popular movement. At first they supported the Girondins, who provided most of the ministers and dominated most of the Assembly's committees.

b) The September Massacres

In August the situation of French armies on the frontier was desperate. Lafayette fled to the Austrians on 17 August. With a leading general deserting, who could still be trusted? Panic and fear of treachery swept the country. This was increased when the Prussians crossed the French frontier and captured Longwy. By the beginning of September, Verdun, the last major fortress on the road to Paris, was about to surrender.

The Commune called on all patriots to take up arms: thousands volunteered to defend the capital and the Revolution. But once they had left for the front there was concern about the overcrowded prisons, where there were many priests and nobles, counter-revolutionary suspects. A rumour arose that they were plotting to escape, kill the helpless population and hand the city over to the Prussians. Marat, a powerful figure in the Commune, called for the conspirators to be killed. The massacre of prisoners began on 2 September and continued for five days. Between 1100 and 1400 of the 2600 prisoners in Paris jails were murdered. Only a quarter were priests and nobles: the rest were common criminals. The killers were the *sans-culottes* of the Sections. The Commune made no attempt to stop them, nor did any of the other authorities. This would have meant mobilising the National Guard and risking another Champ de Mars.

The massacre cast a shadow over the first meeting of the Convention. Most deputies from the provinces were shocked by the killings and rallied to the Girondins. The hatred of the Girondins for the Jacobins and for their *sans-culotte* supporters was intensified. From now on, moderates and foreign opinion regarded Montagnards and *sans-culottes* as blood-thirsty savages – *buveurs de sang* (drinkers of blood).

Just as the fortunes of war had brought about the September Massacres, they also brought an end to this part of the Terror. On 20 September at Valmy 52 000 French troops defeated 34 000 Prussians. This had great significance. If the Prussians had won, there is little doubt that Paris would have fallen. This would probably have meant the end of the Revolution.

Brunswick, the Prussian commander-in-chief, retreated to the frontier and French armies took the offensive again. Within a month they had occupied much of the left bank of the Rhine. In November Dumouriez defeated the Austrians at Jemappes and occupied most of Belgium. In the south Nice and Savoy were conquered.

The French now began to talk about natural frontiers, the Rhine, Alps and Pyrenees, which meant annexing territory. This was contrary to the policy laid down by the Constituent Assembly in May 1790: 'the French nation renounces involvement in any war undertaken with the aim of making conquest'. Avignon, papal territory in France since 1273, had been annexed in 1791. Now Savoy (November 1792) and

Nice (January 1793) were added to French territory. A revolutionary administration was set up in conquered lands. French armies had to be paid and fed at the expense of the local population. Church lands and those belonging to enemies of the new regime were confiscated. Tithes and feudal dues were abolished. These measures alienated much of the population and confirmed Robespierre's prediction that French armies would not be welcomed abroad.

c) The Trial of Louis XVI

The Jacobins insisted on the trial of the King, in order to establish the republic more firmly. They increasingly depended on the *sans-culottes*, who wanted the King tried and executed, as they held him responsible for the bloodshed at the Tuileries in August 1792. The Girondins tried to prevent a trial and when they were not able to do this they made two attempts to save Louis' life. They proposed that a referendum should be held to decide the King's fate. When the King was found guilty and sentenced to death, they proposed a reprieve.

What sealed the King's fate was Marat's proposal that a decision should be reached by *'appel nominal'* (each deputy was to announce his decision publicly), 'so that traitors in this Assembly may be known'. In an Assembly of 721 deputies, no-one voted that Louis was innocent, while 693 voted that he was guilty. When it came to the sentence 361 voted unconditionally for the death penalty, and 319 for imprisonment. The Convention voted against a reprieve by 387 votes to 334.

The King was executed on 21 January 1793. As Saint-Just, a leading Jacobin, said, he was executed not for what he had done but for what he was: a menace to the Republic. It was the first Jacobin victory in the Convention and left the factions more hostile to one another than ever. Though over half the Girondin leaders, including Brissot, had voted for the death penalty, they were branded as royalists and counter-revolutionaries by the Montagnards. By Louis' execution the Montagnards gained an ascendancy in the Convention which they rarely lost afterwards. Brissot hardly spoke there after the trial.

d) The War Extended

The Convention had thrown down the gauntlet to the European monarchs when, in November 1792, it had decreed that fraternity and assistance would be given to all peoples wishing to regain their liberty. In January 1793 it passed a decree claiming for France the natural frontiers of the Rhine, Alps and Pyrenees. The Great Powers were alarmed at the annexation of Nice and Savoy and Britain was particularly concerned at the Rhine becoming a natural frontier for France. This would involve the annexation of a large part of the United Provinces as well as the whole of Belgium. William Pitt, the British Prime Minister, was determined that both of these should be kept out of French hands. They were seen as the key to British security, not only in the Channel but also on the routes to India (as the Dutch possessed the Cape of Good Hope and Ceylon). The British also disliked the French re-opening the River Scheldt to navigation (its closure since 1648 had led to the decline of the port of Antwerp as a rival to London).

The French misunderstood the situation in Britain. They did not realise that the reform movement there was not revolutionary. They mistakenly thought that there would be a revolution in Britain. They also thought that in war Britain would crumble as Prussia and Austria had done at Valmy and Jemappes. The British, for their part, thought that France was bankrupt and on the verge of civil war. Each side thought the war would be short and easy and entered into it lightly. The Convention unanimously declared war on Britain and Holland in February 1793, and on Spain in March.

To the surprise of the French the war went badly. Dumouriez was defeated by the Austrians at Neerwinden in March. He therefore decided to march on Paris, dissolve the Convention and restore the Constitution of 1791 and the monarchy. When his army refused to follow him, he deserted to the Austrians with the Duc de Chartres – the future King Louis Philippe and son of the Duc d' Orléans (now known as Philippe Égalité). The defection of Dumouriez, who had enjoyed the enthusiastic backing of the Girondins, further weakened the Girondins' position in the Convention and within the Paris clubs. Meanwhile, the French lost Belgium and the left bank of the Rhine and there was fighting once again on French soil. At the same time there was civil war in the Vendée.

e) The Effects of the War

By the winter of 1792–3 the counter-revolution in France had virtually collapsed. It was revived by the expansion of the war and conscription. The government ordered a levy of 30 000 troops in February 1793. This led to a massive rising in four departments south of the Loire in what became known as the 'Vendée militaire' or simply the Vendée.

The troubles in the Vendée had begun long before 1793 and conscription. Peasants there were paying more in land tax than they had under the ancien régime and so disliked the revolutionary government. This dislike turned into hatred with the Civil Constitution of the Clergy (see pages 50–1). It had been strongly resisted in the area and there were many non-jurors. The sale of church lands was also unpopular, because most were bought by the bourgeoisie of the towns, who often raised rents. Those who bought biens became supporters of the Revolution, which was a guarantee they could keep the land. Those who were not successful became hostile to the government. The peasants looked to the nobles as their natural leaders. Many of these were monarchist, so the rising became caught up in counter-revolution. New local officials, constitutional priests and National Guards were massacred. The situation was so serious that in May the government had to withdraw 30 000 troops from the front to deal with the rising. Yet the rebels were never a serious threat to the government in Paris. They were ill-disciplined – better at guerrilla warfare than set-piece battles – and unwilling to move far from their homes.

Economic problems, for which the war was largely responsible, added to the difficulties of the government. To pay for the war more and more *assignats* were printed and they had fallen to half their nominal value by February 1793. This pushed up prices. The harvest in 1792 was good but bread was scarce. Saint-Just pointed out why in a speech in November 1792: 'The farmer does not want to save paper money and for this reason he is most reluctant to sell his grain'. The results of high prices and scarcity were, as usual, widespread riots and demands from the *sans-culottes* for price controls and requisitioning.

The support of the people was necessary to fight the war, so it was clear that some of their demands would have to be granted. This was realised first of all by the Montagnards. And just as the Montagnards were drawing closer to the *sans-culottes*, the Plain was drawing closer to the Montagnards. Its members shared the Girondin hatred of Robespierre and Marat but they held the Girondins responsible for the failures in the war (Dumouriez had been closely associated with them), the rising in the Vendée and the economic crisis. After all, several ministers were Girondins. The Plain, therefore, joined the Montagnards in favour of repressive measures. Barère, a leader of the Plain, told the Convention that it should recognise three things: in a state of emergency no government could rule by normal methods; the bourgeoisie should not isolate itself from the people, whose demands should be satisfied; the bourgeoisie must retain control of this alliance, and so the Convention must take the initiative by introducing the necessary measures.

*These measures were passed by the Convention between 10 March and 20 May 1793. They had three objectives: to watch and punish suspects, to make government more effective and to meet at least some of the economic demands of the *sans-culottes*. On 10 March a Revolutionary Tribunal was set up in Paris to try counter-revolutionary suspects and was intended to prevent massacres like those of September 1792. 'Let us embody Terror', said Danton in the debate on the decree, 'so as to prevent the people from doing so'. This tribunal was to become one of the main agencies of the Terror.

Owing to the resistance to conscription and the suspicion of generals after Dumouriez's defection, representatives-on-mission were sent to the provinces. They had almost unlimited powers over the department administrations and the armies. They were deputies of the Convention, mainly Montagnards, whose job was to speed up conscription and keep an eye on the conduct of generals, whom they could arrest. This was the first stage in reasserting central control over the provinces, which had been dismantled in the local government reforms.

Plots were blamed for the rising in the Vendée, so *comités de surveillance* (surveillance or watch committees, sometimes known simply as revolutionary committees) were set up in each commune and each section of major towns. They were to keep an eye on foreigners and suspected traitors, and they provided many victims for the Revolutionary Tribunal. Severe measures were to be taken against rebels. The summary execution decree provided for the trial and execution of armed rebels within 24 hours of capture. These trials were held without a jury and there was no appeal. They condemned many more victims than the Revolutionary Tribunal itself. Draconian laws were also passed against *émigrés*. Their property was confiscated and they were to be executed if they returned to France.

*On 6 April perhaps the most important of all these measures, the Committee of Public Safety was set up to supervise and speed up the activities of ministers, whose authority it superseded. The Committee was not a dictatorship: it depended on the support of the Convention, which renewed its powers each month. Who was to be on the new Committee? Danton, supported by the Plain, wanted a committee without extremists. Thus of the nine members selected in April, seven, including Barère, were from the Plain. There were only two members from the Mountain, of whom Danton was one, and no Girondins at all. Danton and Robespierre spoke of the need for winning the support of the people for the Republic. This could be done by economic concessions. On 4 May a maximum price, which the Girondins opposed, was fixed for grain and later in the month a compulsory loan was imposed on the wealthy.

All these measures – Revolutionary Tribunals, representatives-on-mission, watch committees, the Committee of Public Safety and the summary execution decree – were to become vital ingredients of the Terror. At first they were applied only partially, if at all, outside the Vendée.

f) The Fall of the Girondins

Danton and other Montagnards had asked the Girondins to stop attacking Parisian *sans-culottes* as *buveurs de sang* but to no avail. On 26 May Robespierre came down on the side of the *sans-culottes* when he invited 'the people to place themselves in insurrection against the corrupt [Girondin] deputies'. On 31 May a rising began which spread rapidly when news of the overthrow of the Jacobins in Lyon reached Paris on 1 June. On 2 June 80 000 National Guardsmen surrounded the Convention and directed their cannon at it. They demanded the expulsion of Girondins from the Assembly and a maximum price on all essential goods. When the deputies tried to leave they were forced back. For the first time armed force was being used against an elected parliament. To avoid a massacre or a revolutionary commune seizing power, the Convention was compelled to agree to the arrest of 29 Girondin deputies and two ministers.

g) The New Committee of Public Safety

After 2 June most deputies feared and distrusted the Montagnards. However, they did not want to see the Republic overthrown by domestic or foreign enemies and so for the next 14 months they were reluctant accomplices of the Jacobin minority. When a new Committee of Public Safety was formed between July and September 1793, the 12 members were all either Montagnards, or deputies of the Plain who had joined them. All were middle class, except for Hérault de Séchelles, who was a former noble. Eight of them were lawyers, two were engineers. Nearly all were young: the average age was just 30. There was no chairman: all the members were jointly responsible for the Committee's actions.

The new Committee was to become the first strong government since the Revolution began. Barère became the spokesman of the Committee in the Convention. Carnot, an engineer, devoted his considerable energy and organising ability to the army, qualities which led Napoleon to call him 'the organiser of victory'. In September, owing to *sans-culotte* pressure, two members of the Cordeliers Club, Collot d'Herbois and Billaud-Varenne, joined the Committee. Robespierre's closest associates on the Committee were Couthon, who was paralysed and confined to a wheel-chair, and Saint-Just. Proud and courageous, Saint-Just was to be a leading advocate of Terror. All the members were re-elected to the Committee by the Convention every month from September 1793 to July 1794, except for Hérault. He retired from the Committee in December 1793 and was executed with Danton in April 1794. These members did not share the same opinions but they were prepared to forget their differences in order to deal with the pressing problems which faced France.

Maximilien Robespierre joined the Committee on 27 July. Owing to his influence in the Jacobin Club and the Commune he was expected to provide a link between the middle class Jacobins and the *sans-culottes*. He never had much support in the Convention and many could not stand his narrow self-righteousness. Oelsner, a German member of the Jacobin Club, wrote of him: 'I know no-one so insufferable, so arrogant, so taciturn, so boring'. Pétion, the Mayor of Paris, summed up what many thought :

1 Robespierre is extremely touchy and suspicious; he sees plots, treason . . . everywhere . . . Imperious in his opinions, listening

only to himself, intolerant of opposition, never pardoning those who had wounded his *amour-propre*, never admitting his mistakes.

Yet he was known as 'the Incorruptible' because he did not seek power or wealth for himself and was consistent in putting the good of the country above all other considerations. Some have described him as 'a moral fanatic', because his love of *vertu* swept aside all human feelings, as when he wrote:

1 The spirit of the Republic is virtue, in other words love of one's country, that magnanimous devotion that sinks all private interests in the general interest.

To him principles were everything, human beings nothing. Anyone who did not put '*vertu*' first would have to be sacrificed:

1 Terror is nothing other than justice, prompt, severe and inflexible; it is therefore an emanation of virtue . . . Break the enemies of liberty with terror, and you will be justified as founders of the Republic.

His steely adherence to some principles did not prevent Robespierre from being an extremely astute politician. He usually acted with caution, waiting for the right moment and showed remarkable flair for choosing it. After Varennes he had advised against republican demonstrations, because they would give the authorities an excuse for crushing the radicals. He associated himself with the risings of 10 August 1792 and 2 June 1793 only at the last minute, when he knew they would be successful. He was to show the same skill in revolutionary government, isolating his rivals from their sympathisers before crushing them.

It was Robespierre's tactical skill which led him to ally with the *sans-culottes*. He saw the need for the Montagnards to be allied to the people if the Revolution was to survive. During the rising of 31 May – 2 June he wrote in his diary:

1 What is needed is one single will . . . The danger within France comes from the middle-classes and to defeat them we must rally the people.

His championship of the people did not begin here but went back to the time when he was a lawyer in Arras before the Revolution. He had derived from Rousseau his belief in the sovereignty of the people and his ideal of a republic of small property-owners. He was known as the poor man's advocate when he was elected to the Estates-General in 1789, where he soon distinguished himself as a liberal and champion of the Rights of Man. He opposed the division of citizens into 'active' and 'passive' and the laws which deprived West Indian negroes of full civil rights. His economic ideas were similar to those of the *sans-culottes*. Like them he disapproved of excessive wealth and told the Convention in April 1793 that 'the extreme disparity between rich and poor lies at the heart of many of the troubles and crimes of our society'. The common ideal of both Robespierre and *sans-culottes* was that of small, independent producers, peasants and artisans, each owning his field or workshop. This ideal was in conflict with capitalism's belief in the concentration of industry. He did not believe in the equal distribution of property, yet he felt that the state had the obligation 'to provide for the subsistence of all its members, either by providing work for them or by providing the means of subsistence for those unable to work'.

As Robespierre shared many ideas with the *sans-culottes* he was popular with the people of Paris but he was never one of them. He dressed with the silk stockings, knee-breeches and powdered wig of the old regime. He never took part in a demonstration and was never carried shoulder-high by the people, as Marat was. Robespierre was a rather remote figure who lived comfortably, though not ostentatiously, in the *petit-bourgeois* household of the cabinet maker Duplay.

h) The Federal Revolt

The Committee of Public Safety found itself confronted by massive problems. One of the most serious was a revolt in the provinces. Many departments resented the influence of Paris and its Commune over the Convention and there were anti-Jacobin movements in Bordeaux, Lyon and Marseille before 2 June 1793. The *journée* of that day extended the movement considerably: 60 departments protested against the expulsion of the Girondins although there was serious resistance to the Convention in only eight. The Montagnards called these revolts 'federalism' and said that they were royalist plots to destroy the unity of the Republic. In fact both sides believed in the unity of the Republic and the revolts had, initially, nothing to do with royalism or counter-revolution. But the revolution in Toulon went further than intended, as the government cut off food supplies to the city. To obtain food the town authorities negotiated with the British, who insisted that the monarchy be proclaimed. British troops entered the town on 28 August. As half the French fleet was lying off the coast at Toulon, this was a most serious blow to the republic.

Once the towns of Marseille, Lyon and Toulon had rejected the Convention, many smaller towns in the Rhône valley and Provence followed suit. Federalism appeared a serious threat to the government, which had to face clerical opposition and hostility to conscription, despite the fact that 'federal' forces were pitifully small. Marseille was able to raise only 3500 men, Bordeaux 400, and none of them wanted to move far from home. There was little cooperation between the centres of revolt. Each was concerned only with its own local problems and was indifferent to what happened elsewhere. This failure to cooperate enabled the government to pick off the rebel areas one by one.

Another problem facing the government was that the war against the allies continued to go badly in the summer of 1793. The Austrians pushed into France. The Spaniards invaded Roussillon in the south. The allies had 160 000 men on the Netherlands' border with France, with a smaller French force opposing them. If York and Coburg, the allied commanders, had joined forces and moved on Paris the French would have faced disaster. Fortunately for them, the allies did not coordinate their plans. Pitt ordered the Duke of York to capture Dunkirk as a naval base, so he turned west. The Austrians turned east, and the allied army broke in two. This enormous blunder saved France.

The disunity of the allies at this time was a major factor in France's survival. Prussia and Austria were quarrelling about Poland: the second partition took place in 1793, in which Austria gained nothing. As Austria feared that Russia and Prussia would take even more territory in Poland, she was unwilling to commit herself fully in the west. She turned her attention to the Austrian Netherlands, which she wanted to exchange for Bavaria, as this would make her territories more compact. Prussia feared such a strengthening of Austria's power, and so ordered her generals not to take the offensive against France.

2   The Dominance of the *Sans-culottes*

The power of the *sans-culottes* was a product of the war. They had played an important role in the Revolution in 1789 by storming the Bastille and in bringing the King to Paris in the October Days, but after that the bourgeois National Guard was used to keep them under control, as it did at the Champ de Mars. The first opportunity for *sans-culotte* militants came with the opening of the National Guard to 'passive' citizens in July 1792. They overthrew the monarchy and from the summer of 1792 to the spring of 1794 no-one could control Paris without obtaining their support. They were responsible for the *journée* of 31 May – 2 June 1793 which brought the Jacobins to power.

a) Their Ideas and Organisation

The *sans-culottes* hated the aristocracy and anyone of great wealth and had a fierce devotion to equality. They did not say '*monsieur*' but '*citoyen*' and used the familiar '*tu*' instead of the polite '*vous*'. Their red caps, originally associated with freed slaves, symbolised the equality of all citizens. Anyone with a haughty or scornful attitude was labelled an 'aristocrat'. They were passionately anti-clerical because priests had joined with aristocrats in taking the wealth created by ordinary men and women. Along with their desire for equality went a belief in direct democracy. For the *sans-culottes* the sovereignty of the people could not be delegated to representatives. The people had the right to control and change their elected representative at any time and if they were betrayed they had the right of insurrection. Political life must take place in the open: the patriot had no reason to hide his opinions. The meetings of the Assembly must therefore be open to the public and deputies must vote aloud.

The majority of *sans-culottes* were wage-earners but they were not the ones who held power in the Sections. Each Section was controlled by a small minority of militants, who were usually the better-off members, because they had the time to devote to Section business. Of the 454 members of the Revolutionary Committees in Paris in 1793–4 65 per cent were shopkeepers, small workshop masters and independent craftsmen; 26 per cent were *rentiers*, civil servants and members of the liberal professions; only eight per cent were wage-earners. They exercised power through their own institutions, which were not responsible to the central government. The Commune and the Sections were the administrative units of Parisian local government, with their officials and elected committees. They had their own police and armed forces, as they controlled the National Guard. They also controlled the popular societies. These were encouraged by the government as long as there was danger from internal and foreign foes, as they helped the war effort, kept a watch on suspects and assisted representatives-on-mission in purging local authorities. In 1793 they were often more important than the municipalities, as they issued 'certificates of citzenship', without which no-one could be employed.

The Parisian *sans-culottes* had the force with which to seize power but they chose to persuade or intimidate the Convention, never to replace it. They wholeheartedly supported the government on basic issues, such as in their hatred of the aristocracy and in their determination to win the war.

b) Concessions to the *Sans-culottes*

The *sans-culottes* had put the Jacobins in power, so a new Constitution, which recognised many of their aspirations, was rushed through the Assembly in June 1793. It was preceded by a Declaration of Rights, which went much further than that of 1789, as it stated the rights of people to work, to have assistance in time of need and to be educated. The right of insurrection, one of the *sans-culottes'* most cherished beliefs, was proclaimed. All adult males were to have the vote and there were to be direct elections.

More soldiers were needed to fight the war, so the Sections also demanded conscription. This came with the *levée en masse* in August 1793. The task for the Committee of Public Safety was enormous. The first class of conscripts, unmarried men between 18 and 25, was nearly half a million. They had to be fed, armed and trained, so all the human and material resources of the nation were put at the government's disposal. State factories were set up to make arms and ammunition. Raw materials were controlled: church bells were melted down for cannon and religious vessels for coinage. The government also took over the control of foreign trade and shipping. The resources for economic planning did not really exist, yet the controlled economy harnessed the energies of the nation on an unprecedented scale. It was remarkably successful in the short-term: without it victory would have been impossible.

c) The *Journée* of 4–5 September 1793

The economic situation continued to deteriorate in the summer. In mid-August the *assignat* was below a third of its face value and drought reduced the grain imports into Paris by three-quarters. One group demanding ruthless action to combat the shortages were the *Enragés*, and their spokesman Jacques Roux. As a priest, in one of the poorest quarters of Paris, Roux was shocked by what he saw: people starving in crowded attics; unemployed, who had worked in the former luxury trades, with large families and no relief. These were people for whom the Revolution had done nothing. His followers were not householders or *sans-culotte* militants but wage-earners, casual labourers, the poor and unemployed. He wanted the Convention to do something about starvation and poverty and when it did nothing, he denounced it. His programme was economic Terror, the execution of hoarders who pushed up the price of grain and a purge of ex-nobles from the army. Robespierre hated him and wanted to destroy him, because he was threatening the Commune and the Convention with direct action in the streets. Roux was arrested, and died in prison in February 1794.

On 4 September a crowd gathered before the *Hôtel de Ville* to demand bread and higher wages and on 5 September it marched on the Convention. This could have ended in a *coup* like that of 2 June, when Girondin deputies were arrested. The Convention avoided this by accepting a series of radical measures. The Sections imposed on the Convention the proclamation of 'Terror as the order of the day'.

One instrument of the Terror the Convention immediately authorised was the formation of a Parisian *'armée révolutionnaire'*. Subsequently, 56 other armies, unauthorised, were set up in the provinces between September and December 1793, and were used in about two-thirds of the departments. These civilian armies were to ensure the food supplies of Paris and the large provincial cities, and round up deserters from the army, hoarders, refractory priests, religious 'fanatics', political suspects and royalist rebels. The armies were also to mobilise the nation's resources for the war effort by confiscating church silver and bells. They were to establish revolutionary 'justice' in the areas of the south and west, which had shown little enthusiasm for the Revolution.

There were about 6000 in the Parisian *armée révolutionnaire* plus 1200 artillery men, and 30 000 in the provincial armies. Few of their members were wage-earners: the majority were *sans-culotte* militants – shopkeepers and craftsmen. The operation of the Parisian army extended over 25 departments. Their main task, which occupied two-thirds of their forces, was to ensure the capital's food supplies by requisitions in the great grain-producing areas of the north. The other main task of the Parisian army, which occupied a third of its men, was to take part in the savage repression of the federal revolt at Lyon. Another activity, in which both the Parisian and provincial armies engaged, was dechristianisation (see page 84). The Parisian army was remarkably successful in supplying Paris with bread until the spring of 1794, and so helped to preserve the Revolution. The provincial armies also did a good job in supplying major towns and the line army on the eastern frontier. Their success, however, was likely to be short-term, partly because their numbers were small and partly because of the unremitting hostility of the rural population to their work. Yet the joy shown in the countryside when they were disbanded was an indication of just how successful they had been.

The Committee of Public Safety did not like the revolutionary armies because they were anarchic and outside the control of the authorities. They also disliked them because they created opposition to the Revolution by their heavy-handed methods in dealing with the peasants. Robespierre, who had supported the armies up to September 1793, turned against them because of their 'dechristianisation' campaign. The Convention had accepted the Parisian army only with great reluctance and never recognised its counterparts raised in the provinces. They were doomed once the revolutionary government was firmly established.

d) Economic Terror

The Convention had bowed to popular pressure from Roux and the *sans-culottes* in July by passing a law which made death the penalty for hoarding. This probably did more harm than good, as merchants refused to carry large stocks, in case they were accused of hoarding, so shortages were made worse. The Convention accepted price control too when it passed the law of the General Maximum on 29 September. The new law fixed the price not only of bread but of many essential goods and services at one third above the prices current in June 1790. There was no point in fixing prices unless wages were also controlled, as they largely determined what prices would be. Wages were fixed at 50 per cent above the level of 1790. When the peasant refused to sell grain at the maximum price, requisitioning was allowed as the only way to feed the towns and the armies.

The Maximum divided the common people against each other. The peasants hated it because it was often below the cost of production, so they avoided it whenever possible. The *sans-culottes* wanted it so that they could afford to live. When they went into the countryside with the *armée révolutionnaire* to enforce the Maximum they clashed with the peasants and the conflict between town and country was exacerbated. The government was in a difficult position, as farmers would simply stop sowing if they could not make a profit. The cooperation of the wealthy peasants, who controlled most of the harvest, was necessary for the government. They were the municipal councillors and tax collectors, who were expected to oversee requisitioning. Thus the Maximum had to be carried out, where there was no local revolutionary army, by the rich in the countryside. To placate them the government revised prices upwards in February 1794, much to the disgust of the *sans-culottes*.

The government's measures were successful in the short-term. The towns and armies were fed and the *assignat*, worth 22 per cent of its face value in August, rose to 48 per cent in December 1793.

e) The Political Terror

The Terror took three forms. There was the official Terror, controlled by the Committees of Public Safety and of General Security, which was centred in Paris and whose victims came before the Revolutionary Tribunal. There was the Terror in the areas of federal revolt, where the worst atrocities took place. There was also the Terror in other parts of France, which was under the control of watch committees and representatives-on-mission, and the revolutionary armies.

The Committees, mainly the Committee of General Security, were responsible for bringing cases before the Revolutionary Tribunal in Paris. Up to September 1793 the Tribunal had heard 260 cases and pronounced 66 death sentences (26 per cent of the total). For Robespierre and the Montagnards Terror had to be legal and controlled by the government. In staging a series of celebrity trials they were giving way to popular demands but also getting rid of people they genuinely regarded as enemies of the Republic. Now what mattered was the decision to prosecute, as the verdict was automatic – death. Acquittal would have been regarded as a vote of no confidence in the government. The Revolutionary Tribunal became the scene of endless trials and death sentences: Marie Antoinette on 16 October, 31 Girondin deputies on 31 October, Philippe Égalité on 6 November and Mme Roland, wife of the Girondin ex-minister, three days later.

The federal revolt had been put down by the regular army everywhere by the end of the year. Between August and December 1793 Marseille, Lyon and Toulon were taken and the Vendéan rebels crushed. A terrible repression followed everywhere. General Wester-mann informed the Committee of Public Safety: 'The Vendée is no more . . . It has died beneath our sabres, together with its women and children . . . I have crushed the children under my horses' hooves, massacred the women – they, at least, will not give birth to any more brigands.' From January to May 1794 troops moved through the area, shooting almost every peasant they met, burning their farms and crops and killing their animals. Women were raped and mutilated. When the 'pacification' was over, the Vendée was a depopulated desert. Thousands who surrendered crammed the prisons. They could not be released in case they joined the rebels again, so they too were shot without trial – 2000 near Angers alone. In the Vendée 7000 were condemned by revolutionary courts, half the total for the whole of France. Most of these were peasants; hardly any were bourgeois.

Representatives-on-mission were often responsible for the worst atrocities. At Nantes, Carrier carried out the dreadful '*noyades*' (drownings). About 1800 people, nearly half of them women, were put in barges, which were taken to the mouth of the Loire and sunk. In Toulon 800 were shot without trial and a further 282 were sent to the guillotine by a Revolutionary Commission. Lyon was the second city in France and was to pay dearly for its rebellion. Couthon had directed the siege at Lyon and felt that only moderate repression was needed. Robespierre, however, wanted 'inexorable severity', as humane measures would simply encourage new conspiracies. Couthon was replaced by Collot and Fouché, aided by a detachment of the Parisian revolutionary army. People were mown down by cannon fire in front of previously dug graves and many others were guillotined, about 1900 in all. It was in these rebel areas of the west and south-east, which covered only five departments, that 70 per cent of total executions during the Terror took place. Even here, they were confined to limited areas: there were hundreds of executions at Nantes but hardly a dozen at nearby Rouen.

The Terror was carried to other parts of France by representatives-on-mission and revolutionary armies. The representatives were fanatical Jacobins, who packed the new revolutionary committees with their supporters. The government had delegated its powers, under the Law of Suspects of September 1793, to these committees. They could arrest anyone they thought was a danger to the Republic and imprison him indefinitely without trial. A mass arrest of suspects took place (about half a million according to one estimate, of whom 10 000 died in prison). The committees could also send offenders before one of the Revolutionary Tribunals, and purge the local administration, removing moderates and replacing them by *sans-culotte* militants. These committees symbolised the Terror at the local level. By the end of 1793 most rural communes had one. They were the one permanent institution of the Terror in the countryside.

*In many rural areas there was little enthusiasm for the Republic.

Saint-André, a member of the Committee of Public Safety, reported from the Lot that grass-roots democracy had produced communes which were indifferent or hostile to the Revolution. Support for it would have disappeared completely in most parts of France without the representatives, the clubs and the watch committees. Even so, local Jacobins often did not enjoy much support. At Estaing (Aveyron) they could raise only two dozen supporters out of a population of 900. One study of the Terror has estimated that there were 17 000 official executions, 16 per cent of them in Paris and most of the rest in areas of revolt (52 per cent in the Vendée and 19 per cent in the south-east). Of the victims 28 per cent were peasants, mainly from the Vendée and 31 per cent were urban workers, especially from Lyon and Marseille. If one adds the people executed without trial or who died in prison, the number is probably around 50 000.

f) Dechristianisation

Dechristianisation was an attack on the Church which took various forms. Churches were closed, church bells and silver removed, roadside shrines and crosses destroyed and priests were sometimes forced to marry. There were few non-juring priests left in France by late 1793, so the dechristianisation movement became an attack on the constitutional Church, which had failed to persuade the peasants to support the Revolution. Many constitutional clergy supported the Lyon rising, so dechristianisation became part of the struggle against counter-revolution. Although the Convention was unsympathetic to Catholicism and to priests, it connived at the attack on the Church rather than encouraged it.

In October a new revolutionary calendar was introduced to replace the Christian calendar. The new calendar was dated from 22 September 1792, when the Republic was proclaimed. Thus the period from 22 September 1792 to 21 September 1793 became Year 1. The year was divided into twelve months of 30 days, with five supplementary days (soon called *sans-culottides*). Each month was divided into three periods of ten days, every tenth day (*decadi*) being a day of rest. Another decree gave each month a name appropriate to its season: thus Vendémiaire (the month of vintage) ran from 22 September to 21 October, Floréal (the month of flowers) from 20 April to 19 May. The new calendar ignored Sundays and festivals of the Church.

The main impulse for the dechristianisation campaign came from the *sans-culottes* in the Paris Commune and the revolutionary armies, and from the representatives-on-mission. They hated Catholicism, which they felt had betrayed the Revolution. Like the abolition of the monarchy, the destruction of churches was a symbol of their determination to destroy everything connected with the old regime. The Paris Commune stopped paying clerical salaries in May 1793 and in November ordered that all churches in Paris should be closed. Notre Dame became a Temple of Reason. This movement spread rapidly throughout France. By the spring of 1794 most churches in France had been closed. The most enthusiastic dechristianisers were representatives like Fouché, who placed signs above the entrance to cemeteries which read 'Death is an eternal sleep'.

Priests were forced to renounce their priesthood and many were compelled to marry. Estimates of the number of priests who gave up their calling vary from about 6000 (ten per cent of all constitutional priests) to 20 000. This brutal attempt to uproot centuries of Christian belief was deeply resented in the villages. For many ordinary people outside the civil war zones and the main communication routes, dechristianisation, which left large areas of France without priests, was the aspect of the Terror which most affected them.

3 The Dictatorship of the Committee of Public Safety

Towards the end of 1793 the government was overcoming the problems which had threatened the existence of the Republic. The federal revolts had been crushed, the towns were being fed and the *assignat* was rising in value. In the war French armies were doing well. By the end of September they had driven the Spanish armies out of Roussillon and the Piedmontese out of Savoy. The British were defeated at Hondschoote in the same month and the Austrians at Wattignies in October. With renewed confidence the Convention's Committees could now begin to claw back much of the power which had passed to the *sans-culottes* and their organisations.

A conflict between the government and the *sans-culottes* was inevitable at some time. There was administrative anarchy in the departments in the autumn of 1793 as local revolutionary committees, revolutionary armies and representatives like Fouché interpreted the law, or ignored it, just as they pleased. No government can tolerate anarchy indefinitely, yet it had to act carefully. It needed the *sans-culottes* to help requisition food and, as there were no political parties, the Committees relied on the popular societies to make known government instructions and propaganda. The Committee of General Security had to entrust the running of the Terror to local men in the surveillance committees.

The first steps to tame the popular movement were taken in September 1793. The Convention decided that the general assemblies of the Sections could meet only twice a week. In October the Convention passed a decree that government was to be 'revolutionary until the peace'. This meant the indefinite suspension of the Constitution of 1793, which was never put into operation.

a) The Law of 4 December (14 Frimaire) 1793

A major step to central control came with the law of 4 December, accepted by the Plain as much as by the Mountain. The two Committees, whilst deriving their authority solely from the Convention, were given full executive powers. The Committee of General Security was responsible for police and internal security: thus the Revolutionary Tribunal, as well as the surveillance committees, came under its control. The Committee of Public Safety had more extensive powers. In addition to controlling ministers and generals, it was to control foreign policy and purge and direct local government. The chief officials of the communes and departments, who had been elected, were placed under 'national agents' appointed by and responsible to the central government. The representatives-on-mission, sent out by the Convention in April, were now put firmly under the control of the Committee of Public Safety. All revolutionary armies, except that in Paris, were to be disbanded.

This marked the end of anarchy and severely curtailed the power of the *sans-culottes*. It gave France her first strong government since 1787. It also marked a complete reversal of the principles of 1789. Saint-Just was correct when he said that the law was the opposite of revolutionary. The Constitutions of 1791 and 1793 had established decentralisation, elections to all posts, the separation of legislative from executive power and non-political justice. Now all this was changed and many of the characteristics of the *ancien régime* reappeared. Robespierre justified this by saying that a dictatorship was necessary until foreign and internal enemies of the Revolution were destroyed. 'We must', he said, 'organise the despotism of liberty to crush the despotism of kings'. It was contrary to the ideas of democracy and people's rights he had advocated when he had been out of office.

b) The Fall of the Hébertistes

The main danger to Robespierre came from Hébert and his followers. His newspaper *Le Père Duchesne*, which preached extreme violence, was very popular with the *sans-culottes*. Hébert had supported the Jacobins against the Girondins and wanted high office after the *coup* of 2 June 1793. When he failed to become Minister of the Interior he turned against the Jacobins. He accused the Committee of Public Safety of tyranny and tried to obtain power for himself by becoming a champion of popular discontent. The Hébertistes had few supporters in the Convention but many in the Cordeliers Club, the Commune, the Paris revolutionary army and the popular societies. Robespierre disliked them intensely because they took a leading part in the dechristianisation campaign, which turned Catholics against the Revolution. He also disliked their political extremism: their demands that more hoarders should be executed and that there should be a redistribution of property. To isolate them from the masses Saint-Just proposed a decree on 26 February 1793 (8 Ventose) for the confiscation of the property of suspects, which was to go to the poor.

At the beginning of March Hébert announced in the Cordeliers Club that an insurrection was necessary 'that shall bring death to those who oppress us'. Some historians think that Hébert was not attempting to seize power but simply wanted a mass demonstration to put pressure on the government. Whatever he wanted, he was not acting in response to popular pressure and there was little response from the Sections. Robespierre decided the time had come to destroy him. Hébert and 18 supporters were arrested. There was unlikely to be opposition from the Convention, as none of the arrested was a deputy, but there might be disturbances on the streets of Paris. The government, therefore, acted cautiously. It did not arrest the leaders of the Commune, and the Hébertistes were accused of what would discredit them most in the eyes of the *sans-culottes*: of being foreign agents who wanted a military dictatorship, which would prepare the way for a restored monarchy. The populace was taken in by this government propaganda, so that when the Hébertistes were guillotined on 24 March, Paris remained calm.

The Committee took advantage of the situation to make a firmer base for its dictatorship. The Parisian revolutionary army was disbanded, the Cordeliers Club was closed and the popular societies were forced to disband. The Commune was purged and filled with the supporters of Robespierre. Representatives-on-mission, who had been responsible for some of the worst atrocities in the provinces, were recalled to Paris.

c) Danton's Death

Another group in opposition to Robespierre centred round Danton, who wanted to restore freedom to the local authorities by ending the centralisation imposed in December. He also wanted to heal the divisions in the revolutionary movement and end the Terror. He saw that for this to happen the war would have to come to an end, as it was largely responsible for the Terror. He had become very wealthy and it was not clear where his new-found wealth came from. Nearly 400 000 livres spent by the Ministry of Justice when he was in charge could not be accounted for. It appeared that Danton was corrupt. He was accused of being bribed by foreign powers, a damaging accusation which had been levelled at Hébert.

Danton's friend, Camille Desmoulins, supported him in his desire to end the Terror. Desmoulins had asked in his newspaper *Le Vieux Cordelier* as early as December 1793 for the release of '200 000 citizens who are called suspects'. The publisher Nicolas Ruault commented on the situation as it was developing:

1 It is sad to see the patriots destroying each other and thus weakening both their own strength and their cause. Some who have long preached murder and death, who made 'Terror the order of the day', such as Danton and Camille Desmoulins, now
5 feel this so strongly that they are retracing their steps and suggesting 'clemency committees' instead of the revolutionary committees. But the madmen who control the Committee of Public Safety and the National Convention do not listen to them; the scent of the blood they spill gives them courage; they treat
10 Danton and Camille Desmoulins as counter-revolutionaries.
   So far these two are the only ones I can see who are returning to common sense, whose revolutionary frenzy is over, who feel remorse for the past or apprehension for the future; they foresee that all these crimes, these bloody executions, may well turn
15 public opinion against the very revolution it began and has supported.

The Committee of Public Safety regarded Danton as a threat because, unlike Hébert, he had a large following in the Convention. His policies of peace and an end to the Terror would, they felt, leave the door open for a return of the monarchy. He was, therefore, brought before the Revolutionary Tribunal and on 5 April 1794 was executed with many of his followers, including Desmoulins. The Terror now seemed to have a momentum of its own. The members of the Committees had become brutalised and acted vindictively in ways of which they would have been ashamed only two years earlier. Desmoulins' wife tried to organise a demonstration in his support. She was arrested and in April went to the scaffold, along with the wife of Hébert. In no way could they be regarded as presenting a threat to the Committee.

The effect of the fall of Hébert and Danton was to stifle all criticism of the Committee of Public Safety. Everyone now lived in an atmosphere of hatred and suspicion, in which deputies were afraid to say anything, as an incautious word could lead to a death sentence. Thibaudeau, a Montagnard deputy, brilliantly described the situation in his memoirs:

1 The National Convention was itself no more than a nominal parliament, a passive instrument of the Terror. From the ruins of its independence arose that monstrous dictatorship which grew to such fame under the name of Committee of Public Safety. The
5 Terror isolated and stupefied the deputies just as it did ordinary citizens. On entering the Assembly each member, full of distrust,

watched his words and actions lest a crime be made out of them. And indeed everything mattered: where you sat, a gesture, a look, a murmur or a smile.

10   The majority of the Convention was no more terrorist than the majority of the nation. It did not order the *noyades* of Nantes or the *mitraillades* of Lyon. But being unable or afraid openly to criticise that which they inwardly disliked, they maintained a dull silence. The sessions, once so long and stormy, were for the most

15   part calm and unimpassioned and lasted only an hour or two. They could only use the shadow of liberty remaining to them on matters of slight importance and on weighty matters they waited for the initiative to come from the Committee of Public Safety and quietly followed its lead. Its members, its reporter, were awaited

20   like heads of state. . . . The reporter mounted the tribune amidst the most profound silence and. . . . his proposals were always adopted . . . [The Committee] had in fact taken possession of all the powers of legislation and government, thought and action.

d) The Great Terror

The government wanted to be in complete control of repression, so in May 1794 it abolished all the provincial Revolutionary Tribunals. All enemies of the Republic had now to be brought to Paris, to be tried by the Revolutionary Tribunal there. This did not mean that the Terror would become less severe. Though the 'factions' of Danton and Hébert had been crushed, some of their supporters were still alive, so the Terror would have to continue until they were eliminated too. Robespierre was not concerned with protecting the innocent, if this allowed dangerous enemies of the Revolution to escape.

After attempts had been made to murder them both, Robespierre and Couthon drafted the Law of Prairial, which was passed on 10 June 1794. 'Enemies of the people' were defined as 'those who have sought to mislead opinion . . . to deprave customs and to corrupt the public conscience'. These terms were so vague that almost anyone could be included. No witnesses were to be called and judgement was to be decided by 'the conscience of the jurors' rather than by any evidence produced. Defendants were not allowed defence counsel and the only verdicts possible were death or acquittal. This law removed any semblance of a fair trial and was designed to speed up the process of revolutionary justice. In this it succeeded. More people were sentenced to death by the Revolutionary Tribunal in the nine weeks after 10 June than in the previous 14 months of its existence. Many of them were from the upper classes: 38 per cent of nobles, 26 per cent of clergy and nearly half the wealthier bourgeoisie who were victims of the Terror, were executed at this time.

The President of the Tribunal wrote to the Committee of Public Safety: 'Perhaps we should purge the prisons at a simple stroke and rid the soil of liberty of this refuse.' The Committee's response, 'Approved', was signed by Robespierre, Barère and Billaud, though Barère later tried to put all the blame on Robespierre, commenting:

1 Every mind was paralysed by the ascendancy Robespierre had won over the Jacobins and bent beneath the cruel yoke of the terror he had organised. The law was passed by the silence of the legislators rather than by their agreement.

No-one dared to make any criticism of the Committee. 'The Revolution is frozen', Saint-Just commented.

Ruault expressed the general revulsion at the Great Terror, when he wrote:

1 In recent weeks we have seen the deaths of all the greatest and most famous still surviving in France and the richest too . . . all the rest of the Lamoignon family and almost the whole of the *Parlement* of Paris; the famous Lavoisier and almost all his
5 colleagues, the Farmers-General, former members of the Constituent Assembly, such as Le Chapelier, as well as Mme Elisabeth, sister of Louis XVI, etc.
    Who will ever believe that Lavoisier and the others were supporters of slavery or tyranny? No, but they were noble, rich
10 and enlightened; they had to be put to death. The Committee of Public Safety are nothing but . . . *sans-culotte* chieftains. This winter and spring the Committee has done marvels for the good of the state and the defence of the fatherland. It has produced fourteen armies out of nowhere, saltpetre, guns and cannon by
15 the thousand, by the million. But now it is making itself detested by the horror and frequency of executions, which are quite unnecessary. Whatever sort of government may be in power, it has and always will have its critics, people who dislike it. Is that a reason for killing them?

e) Robespierre Loses Support

There is no doubt that Robespierre believed in God, whom he called Providence, who was 'engraved in every pure and feeling heart'. He had a genuine faith in life after death, in which the virtuous would be rewarded. He loathed the dechristianisation campaign of the *sans-culottes*, partly on religious grounds and partly because it upset Catholics and created enemies of the Revolution. He wanted to unite all Frenchmen in a new religion, the Cult of the Supreme Being, which he persuaded the Convention to accept in a decree of 7 May 1794. It began: 'The people of France recognises the existence of the Supreme Being and of immortality of the soul'. This new religion pleased no-one. Catholics were distressed because it ignored Catholic doctrine, liturgy and the Pope. Anti-clericals, including most members of the Committee of General Security, opposed it because they thought it was the first cautious step to reintroduce Roman Catholicism. They felt that Robespierre was setting himself up as the high priest of the new religion.

Robespierre was also losing the support of the popular movement. The *sans-culottes* had become disillusioned by the execution of the Hébertistes, by the dissolution of their popular societies and by the end of direct democracy in the Sections. They were aggrieved also by the raising of the Maximum on prices in March. This led to inflation and by July the *assignat* had fallen to 36 per cent of its face value. When the Commune was under the control of the Hébertistes it had not applied the Maximum on wages, which had risen considerably above the limit allowed. The government decided it would have to act, as the profits of manufacturers were disappearing. On 23 July, therefore, the Commune, now staffed by Robespierre's supporters, decided to apply the Maximum to wages. This led to a fall in wages by as much as a half, and heightened discontent amongst the majority of *sans-culottes*, who were wage-earners, though the employers amongst the *sans culottes* welcomed it.

The Great Terror sickened the population, workers as well as bourgeoisie. After victory in the foreign war it no longer seemed necessary. French armies had taken the offensive in the spring of 1794 and, after defeating the Austrians at Fleurus on 26 June, they recaptured Belgium. All foreign troops were driven from France, as the French moved into the Rhineland and crossed the Alps and Pyrenees.

Yet the dictatorship of the two Committees remained unassailable, until they fell out amongst themselves. In April the Committee of Public Safety set up its own police bureau, with Robespierre in charge, to prosecute dishonest officials. The Committee of General Security deeply resented this interference with its own control of internal security, so that the two Committees became rivals rather than allies. There were conflicts too within the Committee of Public Safety. Some members disliked Saint-Just's laws of Ventose and made sure they were never put into practice. Billaud and Collot had been closely attached to Hébert and so felt threatened by Robespierre, especially Collot, whose excesses at Lyon Robespierre had criticised.

f) Thermidor

At this time of great dissension Robespierre disappeared for over a month from public life. He made no speeches in the Convention between 18 June and 26 July and only two at the Jacobin Club between

11 June and 9 July. He attended the Committee of Public Safety only two or three times and even gave up his work at the bureau of police. It may be that he was worn out, both physically and emotionally, as all the members of the Committee had worked long hours for months without a break. When he did surface it was to address the Convention, not the Committee. On 26 July (8 Thermidor) he abandoned his usual caution and made a speech attacking his colleagues. It was one of his worst speeches, which has been described as the rambling of an exhausted man, who no longer knew where he was going. He finished by saying:

1 Let us recognise that there is a conspiracy against public liberty; that it derives its strength from a criminal coalition intriguing in the heart of the Convention itself; that this coalition has accomplices within the Committee of General Security and its bureaux;
5 . . . that members of the Committee of Public Safety have entered into the plot . . . What is the remedy? To punish the traitors.

When Robespierre was asked to name the men he was accusing, he refused.

Moderates like Carnot and terrorists like Fouché and Collot all felt threatened, so they joined together to plot against Robespierre. When Robespierre attempted to speak on 9 Thermidor (27 July) he was shouted down. The Convention then voted for the arrest of Robespierre, his brother, Couthon and Saint-Just. As they were taken to prisons controlled by the Commune, they were soon released and gathered at the City Hall. The leaders of the Commune now called for an insurrection to support Robespierre and his colleagues. They ordered the National Guard of the Sections, still under their control, to mobilise. However, neither the Jacobin Club nor the Commune could mobilise these militants as they had done on 5 September 1793, because of the dictatorship established by the two Committees. The Committee of General Security now controlled the revolutionary committees of the Sections and the popular societies had been dissolved.

There was great confusion on the evening of 27 July, as the Convention was also calling on the National Guard to support it against the Commune. Most Sections took no action at first: only 16 sent troops to support the Commune. Yet they included some of the famous artillery units and for several hours the Commander of the National Guard had the Convention at his mercy. Only a failure of nerve by him and by Robespierre saved the Convention. Robespierre had no faith in a popular rising for which no plans had been made (most successful *journées* had taken at least a week to prepare) and wanted to keep within the law. Whilst he waited passively, the Convention outlawed those deputies whose arrest they had previously ordered, and the leaders of the Commune. This meant that they could be executed without a trial. The decree of outlawry persuaded many Sections to support the

Convention but when they reached the *Hôtel de Ville* they found there
was no-one defending it. Robespierre was arrested and on 28 July he
and 21 others were executed. In the next few days over 100 members of
the Commune followed Robespierre to the scaffold.

4   The Significance of Robespierre

Historians differ widely in their assessment of Robespierre. Some find
his reputation very difficult to explain. They maintain that he was not
an original thinker but simply expressed ideas that were commonplace
among the Montagnards. He was not a great orator either. His speeches
were always long, repetitive and boring and were delivered in feeble
monotone. He was not an impressive figure like Danton, who could
dominate the Convention by the force of his personality, and has been
described by Richard Cobb as a 'prissy, vaguely ridiculous, prickly
little man . . . no outstanding genius, a consistent winner of second
prizes'.

His supposed power in the Jacobin Club and the Committee of
Public Safety was, it is held, illusory. He never led or controlled either
the Montagnards or the Committee. The Committee did not have a
chairman and all its decisions were taken in common – Robespierre was
simply one of 12 equal members. He was not even the main speaker for
the Committee in the Convention: Barère filled that role. He was,
however, one of only two members of the Committee who never left
Paris (many spent long periods away as representatives-on-mission or,
like Carnot, at the front), and may, therefore, have played a more
prominent role than most in the decisions of the Committee. But there
is no documentary proof of this because the Committee did not keep
minutes of its meetings.

Robespierre certainly had a reputation as the champion of popular
sovereignty and the liberties of the people and he *was* popular. In the
elections to the Convention he came top of the Paris list, gaining more
votes than either Danton or Marat. For some, Robespierre was the
sincere democrat who opposed the distinction between 'active' and
'passive' citizens. He thought that deputies and officials should be both
accountable for their actions and subject to public scrutiny. That is why
he wanted to set up a special police department, which would ensure
that public officials did not abuse their powers. Yet when he was in
office he did nothing to promote social and democratic policies.

Robespierre is sometimes regarded as a bloodthirsty fanatic, dedicated to dispatching all his opponents to the guillotine. The Law of
Prairial, which he and Couthon proposed and which led to the Great
Terror, is put forward as evidence of this. Yet Robespierre protected
the 73 Girondins who had protested against the purge of the Convention on 2 June 1793, when many Jacobins wanted to have them

executed. He publicly condemned the excesses of Collot and Fouché at Lyon, although he had demanded more severity after Couthon's moderate repression.

Contradictions seem to abound in Robespierre's attitudes and actions. Many regarded him as a cautious and calculating politician, who prepared the ground carefully and never took action until he was certain of success. However, a recent study has argued that he was chronically hesitant and tended to disappear from public view or fall sick when there was a major crisis, as he did in the weeks before Thermidor. His unusual boldness at Thermidor was so out of character that historians have explained it as due to mental fatigue and depression. Yet it may be that he took a calculated risk and lost. Right up to the last minute his gamble might have worked.

A good case can be made out for regarding Robespierre as a moderate. There was one criterion which he applied to all that he did: would his actions preserve the Revolution? If extremists were creating enemies of the Revolution, then they must be stopped. He denounced Hébert and the atrocities of representatives-on-mission because they were producing so many opponents of the Republic. He was in favour of relaxing the Maximum in the spring of 1794 because he realised that the regime could not wage war on the whole countryside. He condemned dechristianisation because of its political effects – it turned the peasants against the government. He was even prepared to be surprisingly indulgent towards the weaknesses of others. Private vices could be disregarded when they were not a threat to the regime. He was the most reluctant of all the members of the Committee of Public Safety to sacrifice Danton.

Was Robespierre the great revolutionary who directed events and caused them to take place? Some historians think that he was. It was on his initiative that the Revolutionary Tribunal and Committee of Public Safety were set up and that the Law of Prairial was passed. Though he took no direct part in the *journée* of 2 June 1793, he was the inspiration and guiding hand behind it. The threats to the existence of the Revolution in the spring of 1793 – foreign invasion, civil war and economic crisis – had been removed or brought under control by the end of the year. But this was the work of the Committee as a whole and it appears that other members played a larger part than Robespierre in bringing this about. Carnot, for example, was largely responsible for organising the successful prosecution of the war. It may be that Robespierre is often used as shorthand for the Committee of Public Safety and that when we talk about Robespierre's achievements we should be talking about those of the great Committee.

Robespierre's reputation remains a mystery. 'We still do not know', writes Colin Lucas, 'how this man, who never really held power, managed to build up such a reputation that his name was familiar all over France'.

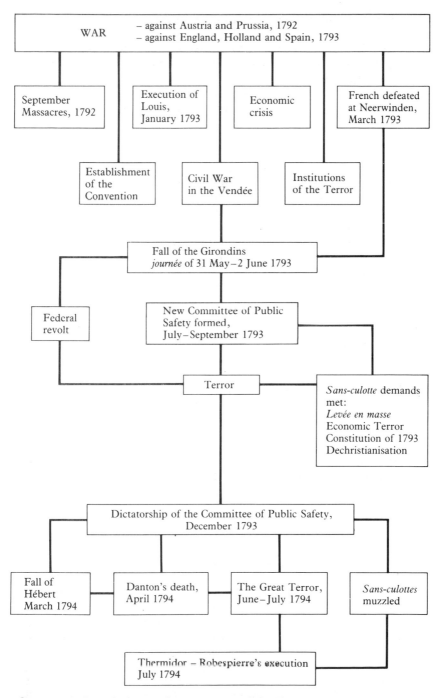

| WAR | – against Austria and Prussia, 1792
 – against England, Holland and Spain, 1793 |

| September Massacres, 1792 | Execution of Louis, January 1793 | Economic crisis | French defeated at Neerwinden, March 1793 |

| Establishment of the Convention | Civil War in the Vendée | Institutions of the Terror |

Fall of the Girondins
journée of 31 May–2 June 1793

| Federal revolt | New Committee of Public Safety formed, July–September 1793 |

| | Terror | Sans-culotte demands met:
 Levée en masse
 Economic Terror
 Constitution of 1793
 Dechristianisation |

Dictatorship of the Committee of Public Safety, December 1793

| Fall of Hébert March 1794 | Danton's death, April 1794 | The Great Terror, June–July 1794 | *Sans-culottes* muzzled |

Thermidor – Robespierre's execution July 1794

Summary – Revolutionary Government and the Terror

Making notes on 'Revolutionary Government and the Terror'

Your notes on the period from September 1792 – July 1794 should help you to understand how and why the Terror came about; what effects the extension of war in 1793 had; how the Committee of Public Safety saved the Revolution and how the *sans-culottes* rose and fell as a political movement. The following headings and sub-headings should help you:

1.   The Struggle for Power: Girondins and Jacobins
1.1.   The Convention
1.2.   The September Massacres, 1792
1.3.   The trial of Louis XVI
1.4.   The war extended, 1793
1.5.   The effects of the war – civil war; economic crisis; military defeats; the machinery of the Terror set up
1.6.   The fall of the Girondins
1.7.   The new Committee of Public Safety
1.8.   The federal revolt
2.   The Dominance of the *Sans-culottes*
2.1.   Their ideas and organisation
2.2.   Concessions to the *sans-culottes*: the Constitution of 1793 and the *levée en masse*
2.3.   The *journée* of 4–5 September 1793 – revolutionary army formed
2.4.   Economic Terror
2.5.   Political Terror
2.6.   Dechristianisation
3.   The Dictatorship of the Committee of Public Safety
3.1.   The Law of 14 Frimaire 1793
3.2.   The fall of the Hébertistes
3.3.   Danton's death
3.4.   The Great Terror
3.5.   Robespierre loses support
3.6.   Thermidor
4.   The Significance of Robespierre

Answering essay questions on 'Revolutionary Government and the Terror'

The period covered by this chapter is the one that A-level examiners seem to like most. Questions usually fall into four groups: 1) the Terror; 2) the Committee of Public Safety; 3) Robespierre; 4) the war. Typical examples are:

1. 'Account for the reign of Terror.'

This is not as simple as it appears, because the Terror was not one event but a series of events, each of which has to be explained. You have to show not only why the Terror began but how and why it changed its character. Make a list of all the different phases of the Terror from 10 August 1792. Now list the reasons for the Terror at each stage. Are there any reasons which are common to all stages of the Terror? Is there one reason above all others which accounts for the Terror and which requires more discussion than the rest?

2. 'Did the success of the Committee of Public Safety in solving France's problems make its downfall certain?'

Draw up a list of the problems which the Committee faced. Opposite each one note if it dealt with the problem successfully and how. Now list the reasons for the downfall of the Committee. What connection do they have with its successes?

3. Robespierre is the only person, except for Louis XVI, about whom you are likely to be asked specifically in questions on the French Revolution. A typical example is:

'Assess the achievements and shortcomings of Robespierre as a revolutionary leader.'

In answering questions like this do not simply enumerate his 'achievements' and his 'shortcomings'. Try to put them in order of importance and then decide whether his successes were more important than his failures and why.

4. Questions on the war are usually on either why it started or what its consequences were. Examples are:

a) 'Why was most of Europe at war with Revolutionary France by the end of 1793?'

In answering this question you will have to discuss the reasons for war beginning in 1792. For this you will have to go back to your notes on the last chapter. As usual, put them in order of importance. Then you will have to do the same again for the extension of war in 1793.

b) 'What were the effects of foreign war on events inside France in the period 1792–99?'

This is a very common question. To answer it you will need information from Chapters 4 and 6 as well as from this one. See also the comments on this question on page 118.

Source-based questions on 'Revolutionary Government and the Terror'

1   The Terror
Read the comments by Ruault on page 88 and by Thibaudeau on pages 88–9. Answer the following questions:
a) Why does Ruault think that Danton and Desmoulins 'are the only ones . . . who are returning to common sense'?
b) Why does Thibaudeau regard the Convention as 'no more than a nominal parliament'?
c) What does he think the deputies 'inwardly disliked' and who were they afraid to criticise?
d) How do Ruault and Thibaudeau show where their sympathies lie?

2   Robespierre
Read the remarks by Robespierre on pages 76–7. Answer the following questions:
a) What does Robespierre mean by 'virtue'?
b) Why does he think that 'the danger within France comes from the middle classes'?
c) What examples can you find of his social ideas?

3   The Great Terror
Read carefully the comments by Ruault on page 90 and then answer the following questions:
a) Which groups of people does Ruault consider to be the main victims of the Great Terror?
b) Why does he think they were executed?
c) Is it true that the members of the Committee of Public Safety were '*sans-culotte* chieftains'?
d) What are the 'marvels' the Committee 'has done . . . for the good of the state'?

CHAPTER 6

The Thermidorian Reaction and the Directory

1 The Thermidorian Reaction

There was a great outburst of delight and relief when Robespierre was executed. Charles de Lacretelle reported the reactions in Paris: 'People were hugging each other in the streets and at places of entertainment and they were so surprised to find themselves still alive that their joy almost turned to frenzy'.

The Thermidorians, as those who helped to overthrow Robespierre were known, were a mixed group – members of the two great Committees, ex-terrorists and deputies of the Plain. The Plain now emerged from obscurity to take control. They were the men who had gained from the Revolution by buying *biens nationaux* or by obtaining government contracts. As regicides they were firmly attached to the Republic and did not want to see the return of a monarchy, even a constitutional one. They also disliked the Jacobins, who had given too much power to the *sans-culottes* and had interfered with a free market. For them popular democracy, anarchy and the Terror were synonymous. They were joined by many Montagnards, which left the Jacobins a small silent minority in the Convention.

a) The Terror Ends

The Terror soon came to an end. Between the end of July 1794 and 31 May 1795, when the Revolutionary Tribunal was abolished, only 63 people were executed, including some who had been leading terrorists. Suspects were released from prison, the law of Prairial was repealed and the Jacobin Club closed. The deputies were determined to gain control of the institutions which had made the Terror possible. This meant abandoning the centralisation established by the Committee of Public Safety. They decreed that 25 per cent of the members of the two Committees had to be changed each month. In August 16 committees of the Convention were set up to take over most of the work of the Committees of General Security and Public Safety. The latter was now confined to running the war and diplomacy. In Paris the Commune was abolished. In local government power passed again to the moderates and property owners, who had been in control before June 1793.

The Thermidorians also decided to grasp the religious nettle by renouncing the Constitutional Church. In September 1794 the Convention decided that it would no longer pay clerical salaries, thus formally separating Church and State for the first time. The free exercise of all religions was guaranteed in February 1795, although all outward signs of rebellion like clerical dress and the use of church bells were forbidden.

b) The Risings of Germinal and Prairial

The Thermidorians wanted to get rid of price controls, partly because they believed in a free market and partly because they were unenforceable. They were abolished in December 1794. Public arms workshops were closed or restored to private ownership. The result was a fall in the value of the *assignat* and massive inflation. The government had to buy its war materials at market prices and had, therefore, to print more *assignats* to pay for them. In August 1794, before the Maximum was abolished, the *assignat* was 34 per cent of its 1790 value. It dropped to 8 per cent in April 1795 and 4 per cent in May. The situation was made worse by a poor harvest in 1794 and a huge increase in the price of bread.

The winter of 1794–5 was one of unprecedented severity. Rivers froze and factories closed down. A combination of economic collapse and the cold produced an enormous increase in misery, suicides and death from malnutrition, as scarcity turned into famine. Ruault described the situation.

1 The flour intended for Paris is stopped on the way and stolen by citizens even hungrier no doubt than ourselves, if such there be within the whole republic. Yet there is no lack of corn anywhere! There is still plenty in store in the departments of the Nord, etc.
5 The farmers absolutely refused to sell it for paper money; you have to go to them and take linen or table silver, jewellery or gold crosses, to get a few bushels.
  Discord sits more firmly than ever within the Convention. Now we are back to where we were at the end of April '93, and a
10 hundred times worse as far as financial matters go. Too many *assignats*, too much government slackness, too much favour shown to enemies of democracy, too much harshness and cruelty to former patriots.

The hungry now included those on fixed incomes: state employees and *rentiers*. They turned their fury against the Convention.

Germinal (1 April) was a demonstration rather than a rising. About 10 000 unarmed people poured into the Convention and demanded bread, the Constitution of 1793 and the release of imprisoned patriots. They expected support from the Montagnards in the Assembly but they did not receive any. When loyal National Guards appeared, the insurgents withdrew without offering any resistance. The repression which followed was light. Barère, Collot and Billaud, all former members of the great Committee of Public Safety, were sentenced to deportation and all known activists during the Terror were disarmed.

Prairial was a much more serious affair. It was an armed rising like those of 10 August 1792 and 2 June 1793. On 1 Prairial (20 May 1795) hunger riots led to an invasion of the Convention by housewives followed by some National Guards. There was complete chaos for three hours, until the Montagnard deputies persuaded the Convention to pass decrees releasing patriots and setting up a Food Commission. In the evening loyal National Guards arrived and cleared the Assembly. The next day about 20 000 National Guards surrounded the Convention. They were opposed by about 40 000 loyal Guards. The Convention's gunners went over to the rebels and aimed their cannon at the Assembly, but no-one was prepared to fire. The rebels presented their petition peacefully and then retired, after the President of the Convention had made some vague promises. On 3 Prairial (22 May) the Convention took the offensive. The rebel suburbs were surrounded by 20 000 troops of the regular army who forced them to give up their arms and cannon. This time the repression was severe: 40 Montagnards were arrested and six were executed. A military commission condemned to death a further 36, including the gunners who had gone over to the rebel side. About 6000 militants were disarmed and arrested. Prairial marked the end of the *sans-culottes* as a political and military force. No longer would they be able to threaten and intimidate an elected assembly. In the Year IV conditions were just about as bad as in the Year III, yet there was no rising. Demoralised, without arms and without leaders, the *sans-culottes* were a spent force.

*Why had they failed? Partly because they were divided – the National Guard of several Sections was loyal to the Convention – partly because there was no institution like the Paris Commune in 1792 to coordinate their activities, and partly because they were politically inexperienced. When they had the advantage and had surrounded the Convention they allowed the opportunity to slip. Some historians see their failure as resulting above all from the loss of support from the radical bourgeoisie, which they had enjoyed from 1789–93. Others see the army as the key factor – the regular army was used against the citizens of Paris for the first time since the Réveillon riots in the spring of 1789. Its intervention was decisive and made clear just how dependent the new regime was on the army. It was not the last time the army would interfere in France's internal politics.

c) The White Terror

The 'White Terror' was an attack on ex-terrorists and all who had done well out of the Revolution by those who had formerly been persecuted. White was the colour of the Bourbons, so 'White Terror' implies that it was a royalist movement. This was true in part, as returned *émigrés* and non-juring priests sought to take advantage of the anti-Jacobin revulsion at the persecution of the Year II. In Nîmes 'Companies of the Sun' were formed by royalists to attack former terrorists. However, most of those who took part in the White Terror were not royalists and had no intention of restoring the *seigneurs* of the *ancien régime* and the Bourbons. Their main concern was vengeance on all those who had been members of the popular societies and watch committees. They were the people who had provided victims for the Revolutionary Tribunals. They also turned against those who had done well out of the Revolution, such as purchasers of *biens nationaux*, constitutional priests and government officials.

The White Terror did not cover the whole of France. It was confined to a score of departments north and west of the Loire and south of Lyon. In Paris it was limited to the activities of the *jeunesse dorée* (gilded youth), sometimes called *'muscadins'* (fops). These were middle class youths – bankers' and lawyers' clerks, actors, musicians, army deserters and sons of suspects or of those executed. They dressed extravagantly with square collars, earrings and long hair turned back at the neck, like those about to be guillotined. They formed gangs to beat up and intimidate Jacobins and *sans-culottes* but there was little bloodshed.

Much more violent was the White Terror in the north-west and south-east. In the Vendée guerrilla warfare revived in 1794 after the brutal repression. In the spring the Chouan movement, opposed to conscription, began in Brittany under the leadership of Jean Cottereau, known as Chouan. Groups of 50 to 100 men were a serious threat to law and order throughout the area, as they attacked grain convoys and destroyed local government outside the towns by murdering officials. From the summer of 1794 to the spring of 1796 they controlled most of Brittany and under royalist leaders sought English support. In June 1795 3000 *émigré* troops were landed at Quiberon Bay and were joined by thousands of Chouans. General Hoche, forewarned, sealed them off with 10 000 troops and compelled them to surrender. 6000 prisoners were taken, including over 1000 *émigrés*: 640 were shot, along with 108 Chouans in the biggest disaster ever suffered by *émigré* forces. The government decided that *Chouannerie* had to be eradicated, and sent Hoche with a huge army of 140 000 to wipe out the Chouan and Vendée rebels. Flying columns were sent across the area north and south of the Loire and by the summer of 1796 they had achieved success.

In the south the murder gangs of the White Terror were not such a threat to the Republic, so little use was made of troops to crush them. This allowed them to become established and to spread rapidly after the disarming of former terrorists and militants. Where the Terror had been at its most savage in Lyon and the Rhône valley, prison massacres reminiscent of the September Massacres in 1792 took place. Gangs of youths, like the *jeunesse dorée* in Paris, killed as many as 2000 in the south-cast in 1795. The killing continued throughout 1796 and for much of 1797.

d) The Constitution of the Year III

The Thermidorians wanted a new constitution, which would guarantee the main features of the Revolution of 1789 – the abolition of privilege, freedom of the individual and the control of local and national affairs by an elected assembly and elected officials. They also wanted to ensure that a dictatorship, like that of the Committee of Public Safety, would be impossible in the future and that there would be no return either to a monarchy or to popular sovereignty on the *sans-culotte* model. Although the Constitution allowed all males over 21, who paid direct taxation, to vote in the primary assemblies, real power was exercised by the electors, whom the primary assemblies elected. The electors chose the deputies and had to pay taxes equivalent to 150–200 days labour. This was so high that the number of electors had fallen from 50 000 in 1790–2 to 30 000. The electors were, therefore, the very rich, who had suffered from the Revolution in 1793–4.

In order to prevent a dictatorship arising, the Thermidorians rigidly separated the legislative from the executive. They also divided the legislative into two chambers, a move which had been deliberately rejected in the Constitution of 1791. There was to be a Council of Five Hundred, all of whom had to be over the age of 30. This Council would initiate legislation and then would pass it on to a Council of Ancients of 250 men over 40. The latter would approve or object to bills but could not introduce or change them. There was no property qualification for the councillors of either chamber. Elections were to be held every year, when a third of the members retired.

The executive was to be a Directory of five, chosen by the Ancients from a list drawn up by the Five Hundred. They would hold office for five years, though one, chosen by lot, had to retire each year. Directors were not allowed to be members of either Council, and their powers were limited. They could not initiate or veto laws or declare war and they had no control over the treasury. Yet they had considerable authority, as they were in charge of diplomacy and the armies and enforced the laws. Ministers (who also could not sit in the Councils) were appointed by and responsible to the directors, as were government commissioners, who replaced the representatives-on-mission and national agents and saw that government policy was implemented in the provinces.

In spite of the complex system of checks and balances designed to prevent a dictatorship, the new Constitution had many weaknesses. The yearly elections promoted instability, as majorities in the Councils could be quickly overturned. There was also no means of resolving conflicts between the legislature and the executive. The Councils could paralyse the Directory by refusing to pass laws which the government required. As the directors could neither dissolve the Councils nor veto laws passed by them, they could overcome the opposition of the Councils only by taking unconstitutional action. The legislature was not in a strong position either, if it clashed with the executive. It could alter the composition of the Directory only by replacing the one director who retired each year with its own candidate. Any change to the Constitution could not take place in less than nine years.

As the Convention knew that it was unpopular and feared that free elections might produce a royalist majority, it decreed that two-thirds of the deputies in the Councils must be chosen from the existing deputies of the Convention.

e) The Rising of Vendémiaire, 5 October 1795

The constitutional monarchists, who wanted a return to a limited monarchy like that in the 1791 Constitution, had been gaining public support, as they seemed to offer a return to stability. They had hoped to put Louis XVI's son, a prisoner in the Temple, on the throne but he died in June. From Northern Italy the Comte de Provence, Louis XVI's brother, immediately proclaimed himself Louis XVIII and on 24 June issued the Verona Declaration. The Declaration was a reactionary document, which made the task of restoring the monarchy more difficult. Louis promised to restore the 'ancient constitution' of France completely, which meant restoring the three orders and the *parlements*. He also promised to restore 'stolen properties', like that of the Church and the *émigrés*. This antagonised all those who had bought *biens nationaux* and all who had benefited from the abolition of the tithe and seigneurial dues. It was a great boost to the Republic.

In the capital open rebellion broke out on 5 October (13 Vendémiaire), when 25 000 armed Parisians gathered to march on the Convention. They greatly outnumbered the 7800 government troops but the latter had cannon, under the command of General Bonaparte, whereas the rebels did not. As over 300 were killed or wounded in the fighting, this was one of the bloodiest of the revolutionary *journées*. It also marked another watershed – the people of Paris would not again attempt to intimidate an elected assembly until 1830.

The divisions among the royalists and the unpopularity of the Verona Declaration all make the rising of Vendémiaire very mysterious. It is usually presented as a royalist rising brought about by the Two-Thirds Decree which, it is said, prevented the royalists from obtaining a majority in the elections to the Councils. Yet the largest groups of rebels were artisans and apprentices: a third of those arrested were manual workers. The rising was not simply against the Two-Thirds Decree but had economic origins too, as many people, including *rentiers*

– small proprietors – and government employees had been badly hit by inflation. A government agent reported on 16 July:

1 The worker's wage is far too low to meet his daily needs; the unfortunate *rentier*, in order to keep alive, has to sell his last stick of furniture . . . the proprietor, lacking other means of subsistence, eats up his capital as well as his income; the civil servant,
5 who is entirely dependent on his salary, also suffers the torments of privation.

These people, who were among the rebels, had supported the Thermidorians and defended the Convention in the risings of Germinal and Prairial.

The repression which followed was light. Only two people were executed, although steps were taken to prevent further risings. The Sectional Assemblies were abolished and the National Guard was put under the control of the new general of the Army of the Interior, Napoleon Bonaparte. For the second time in six months the army had saved the Thermidorian Republic.

2 The Directory

The new third elected to the Council after Vendémiaire and the dissolution of the Convention was mainly royalist, but it was unable to influence the choice of directors. As the Verona Declaration had threatened to punish all regicides, the *conventionnels* elected directors (Carnot was the best known) all of whom were regicides, as this would be a guarantee against a royalist restoration. The directors wanted to provide a stable and liberal government, which would maintain the gains of the Revolution. Yet the problems they faced were daunting. The war appeared to be endless, and it had to be paid for. The treasury was empty, taxes were unpaid and the *assignat* had plummeted in value. Many Frenchmen did not expect the Directory to last more than a few months. However, it did survive and for longer than any of the other revolutionary regimes. This was partly because it was committed to restore the rule of law and because its opponents were discredited. Few wanted a return either to the Jacobin Terror of the Year II or to the absolute monarchy of the *ancien régime*. Many were prepared to accept a constitutional monarchy with limited powers but the royalists were divided amongst themselves. The extremists, who supported the Verona Declaration, hated the constitutional monarchists even more than the republicans. Public apathy also helped the Directory to survive – after six years of revolution and three years of war, revolutionary fervour had all but disappeared. The army supported the Directory as a royalist restoration would mean an end to the war. Army officers did not wish to be deprived of any opportunity provided by war for promotion or plunder. It was the army above all which enabled the Directory to overcome all challenges to its authority, but this was a double-edged weapon. The army which kept the Directory in power would be the most serious threat to its survival, if it became dissatisfied.

a) The Babeuf Plot, 1796

Gracchus Babeuf was one of those who disliked the Constitution of the Year III, because it gave power to the wealthy. He believed that the aim of society should be 'the common happiness', and that the Revolution should secure the equal enjoyment of life's blessings for all. He thought that as private property produced inequality, the only way to establish real equality was 'to establish the communal management of property and abolish private possession'. These ideas were much more radical than those put forward in the Year II and have led many historians to regard Babeuf as the first communist. He was novel too in the way he thought of organising his Conspiracy of Equals. A rising, Babeuf realised, would not come about spontaneously but must be prepared by a small group of dedicated revolutionaries. Through propaganda and agitation they would persuade key institutions like the army and police, who would provide the armed force to seize power, to support them. After seizing power, the revolutionary leaders should not hand it over to an elected assembly but should establish a dictatorship, in order to make fundamental changes in the organisation of society. Marxist historians like Soboul see Babeuf's importance in their theories by arguing that through Buonarotti (a fellow conspirator) his ideas passed to Blanqui in the nineteenth century and thence to Lenin.

Babeuf's importance in the French Revolution itself was slight. His plot to overthrow the Directory was soon revealed by another conspirator. He received no support from the *sans-culottes* and little from former Jacobins. He was arrested in May 1796 and, with one other member of the Conspiracy, was executed a year later.

b) The *Coup d'État* of Fructidor, 1797

The elections of 1797 revealed a growing shift towards the monarchists. People were tired of war abroad and religious conflict at home and found the idea of a constitutional monarchy attractive, believing that it would offer peace and stability. Of the 216 ex-members of the Convention who sought re-election, only 11 were returned. Monarchists won 180 of the 260 seats being contested, bringing their numbers to 330 in the Councils. The wealthy, populous northern departments returned the largest proportion of monarchists, which suggests that the Directory had lost the support of the richer bourgeoisie. The elections, in which fewer than ten per cent of electors voted in some departments, did not give the monarchists a majority in the Councils. However, they did mean that the Directory no longer had majority support and could rely on no more than a third of the deputies. All the monarchists needed to do, it appeared, was to wait for the next elections when more *conventionnels* would have to give up their seats. The monarchists could then obtain a majority and be in a position to restore a monarchy legally. The opponents of the Directory were also successful in elections to the provincial administrations.

The royalists showed their strength when the Councils appointed three of their supporters to important positions. One was elected President of the Five Hundred and another President of the Ancients. Barthélemy, the new director, was regarded as favourable to the monarchists, as was Carnot. Carnot was a moderate, who was prepared to give up conquered territory to make a lasting peace and so was disliked by the generals. This left only two directors who were fervent republicans. They were determined to prevent a royalist restoration and sought help from the army. Bonaparte had already sent Augereau to Paris with some troops to support the republican directors. On the night of 3–4 September 1797 (17–18 Fructidor, Year V) they ordered troops to seize all the strong points in Paris and surround the Council chambers. They then ordered the arrest of two directors, Carnot and Barthélemy, and 53 deputies.

The few deputies who attended the Councils after the *coup* showed that they were thoroughly frightened, when they approved of two laws demanded by the remaining directors. One annulled the elections in 49 departments, removing 177 deputies without providing for their replacement. Normandy, Brittany, the Paris area and the north now had no parliamentary representation at all. A second decree provided for the deportation to Guiana of Carnot (who had escaped and fled abroad), Barthélemy, the 53 deputies arrested and some leading royalists. The directors also annulled the local government elections and made appointments themselves. It was clear to all that this was the end of parliamentary government and of the Constitution of the Year III and that the executive had won an important victory over the legislative. It also meant that the Directory could govern without facing hostile Councils.

After Fructidor the new Directory took action against *émigrés* and refractory priests. *Émigrés* who had returned to France were given two weeks to leave: otherwise they would be executed. During the next few months many were hunted down and were sentenced to death. Clergy were now required to take an oath of hatred for royalty: those refusing would be deported to Guiana. 1400 non-juring priests were sentenced to deportation. However, the Terror which followed Fructidor was more limited than that of the Year II and was not the result of popular enthusiasm. It was carried out solely by the government and the army in an attempt to destroy the royalist movement. In the short-term it succeeded but by alienating Catholic opinion it provided more opponents for the Directory.

c) Financial Reform

Many of the monetary problems of the Directory were due to previous regimes, which had printed more and more *assignats* in order to pay for the war. As these were now almost worthless, in February 1796 the Directory issued a new paper currency, known as *mandats territoriaux*. They too soon lost value, and by July were worth less than five per cent of their nominal value. In February 1797 they ceased to be legal tender.

The monetary crisis had been catastrophic for government officials, *rentiers* and workers, as they saw a rapid decline in what their money could buy. Metal coins now became the only legal currency and these were in short supply: there were only one billion livres in circulation, compared with two and a half billion in 1789. This resulted in deflation, with prices dropping and credit becoming dearer. The inflation of 1795–7 had made the Directory unpopular with the workers. Now it became unpopular with businessmen.

From the *coup* of Fructidor to the spring of 1799 the Directory had little trouble with the purged Councils, so Ramel, the Minister of Finance, took the opportunity of introducing some far-reaching reforms. In September 1797 two-thirds of the national debt was converted into bonds, which could be used to buy national property. This move was of immediate benefit to the government, as it reduced the annual interest on the national debt from 240 million francs (which was about a quarter of government expenditure) to 80 million. It was not of much use to the bondholders. Within a year the value of the bonds had fallen by 60 per cent and soon after that they became worthless, when the government refused to accept them for the purchase of *biens*. This was, in effect, a partial declaration of state bankruptcy, as two-thirds of the national debt was liquidated in this way. The ruin of the *rentiers* was completed but the 'bankruptcy of the two-thirds' helped to stabilise French finances for a time. Aided by the smaller military expenditure when peace with Austria was made, Ramel was able to balance the budget for the first time since the Revolution began.

Ramel wanted to increase revenue as well as to cut expenditure, so in 1798 he established four basic forms of direct taxation: a tax on trading licences, a land tax, one on movable property, and a new one on doors and windows. This was one of the most lasting achievements of the Directory and survived until 1914. At the same time Ramel changed the method of collection, for which locally elected authorities had previously been responsible. Now central control was introduced: commissioners appointed by the directors were to assess and levy taxes.

As there was a continual deficit during wartime, the government had to fall back on practices of the old regime by reviving indirect taxes, although not the hated *gabelle* on salt. The *octrois* was imposed again and was very unpopular, as it raised the price of goods in the towns. Another source of income was plunder from those foreign states, especially in Italy and Germany, which had been occupied by French armies.

d) War: 1794–1799

The battle of Fleurus in June 1794 was the first of a series of successes, which continued until all the members of the First Coalition except Britain had been knocked out of the war. In the summer of 1794 Belgium was occupied and in the following winter the United Provinces were invaded. The French conquered the Rhineland and crossed into Spain. Russia had intervened in Poland, which it was clear would be partitioned again. Prussia therefore made peace with France so that she would be free to claim Polish territory for herself, though she had played little part in the war against France for the last year and a half. At the Treaty of Basle on 6 April 1795, Prussia promised to hand over its territories on the left bank of the Rhine to France. In return she would receive land on the right bank. This treaty freed French troops for an assault on her other enemies. Meanwhile the United Provinces had become the Batavian Republic in January 1795, after a revolt against William V, who fled to England. Having lost Prussian support, the Dutch hastily made peace with France, whose ally they were compelled to become. The French hoped that the powerful Dutch navy would help to tip the naval balance against Great Britain. Spain too made peace in July, giving up to France her part of the island of San Domingo. Of the Great Powers, only Great Britain and Austria remained in the fight against France.

In 1796 the main French objective was to defeat Austria. Carnot drew up the plan of campaign and prepared a pincer movement against Austria. Armies under Jourdan and Moreau would march across Bavaria to Vienna, whilst the armies of the Alps and Italy would conquer Piedmont and Lombardy and then move across the Alps to Vienna. The main attack was to be that of Jourdan and Moreau, who were given 140 000 troops. The Italian campaign, under the 27-year-old General Bonaparte, was to play a secondary role. He had no field experience and had only 30 000 unpaid and ill-disciplined troops. Yet Napoleon was to turn Italy into the major battleground against Austria. He was able to do this by winning the loyalty of his men, to whom he promised vast wealth. Within a month of taking command he had defeated Piedmont and forced her to make peace. In the same month of May he defeated the Austrians at Lodi and entered Milan. Mantua was the key to the passes over the Alps to Vienna, and Napoleon finally captured it in February 1797. The road to Vienna seemed open but all had not been going well for the French. The Archduke Charles had driven Moreau back to the Rhine, so Napoleon signed an armistice with Austria at Leoben in April.

Napoleon decided the terms at Leoben, without consulting the Directory. He was already confident enough to be making his own foreign policy and in doing so ignored specific instructions from the directors. They had wanted to use Lombardy as a bargaining counter to exchange for recognition of French control of the left bank of the Rhine. Napoleon joined Lombardy to Modena and the Papal Legations to form the Cisalpine Republic. Austria recognised Belgium, which the French had annexed in October 1795, as French territory. As compensation for giving up Lombardy and Belgium, Napoleon gave Austria Venice and part of the Venetian Republic, which provided access to the Adriatic. The fate of the left bank of the Rhine was unclear: it was to be decided by a Congress of the Holy Roman Empire. The Directory and the generals on the Rhine were furious that they had to accept what Napoleon had done. As the royalists had won the elections in France, the Directory knew it might need him. The peace of Campo Formio in October 1797 confirmed what had been agreed at Leoben.

Britain was now the only country fighting France. The French wanted to invade Britain, but for this to happen control of the seas was necessary. The French hoped that with the aid of the Dutch and Spanish fleets (Spain had become an ally of France in October 1796) they would be able to obtain this. These hopes were dashed by two British victories in 1797. In February the Spanish fleet was defeated off Cape St. Vincent and the Dutch fleet was almost completely destroyed at Camperdown in October. The war with Britain therefore continued.

*On the continent the prospects for a permanent peace receded, as the French continued to extend their influence. The *coup* of Fructidor removed the two directors, Carnot and Barthélemy, who were prepared to return to France's old frontiers in order to gain a lasting peace. The directors now in control all wanted to keep French conquests and even to extend them. French foreign policy, therefore, became increasingly aggressive. Switzerland was important to France, as it controlled the most important passes to Italy. French troops entered Switzerland in January 1798 to help Swiss Patriots to seize power and turn Switzerland into the Helvetic Republic. Geneva was annexed to France. In Italy the Papal States were invaded and a Roman Republic was set up: the Pope fled to Tuscany. France had many 'sister' republics near her borders: three in Italy – the Cisalpine, Ligurian (which had replaced the Genoese Republic in June 1797) and Roman – plus the Batavian and Helvetic Republics. All were under French influence or control. Meanwhile the French were busy redrawing the map of Germany in negotiations with the Congress of the Holy Roman Empire at Rastatt. In March 1798 the Congress ceded the left bank of the Rhine to France and agreed that

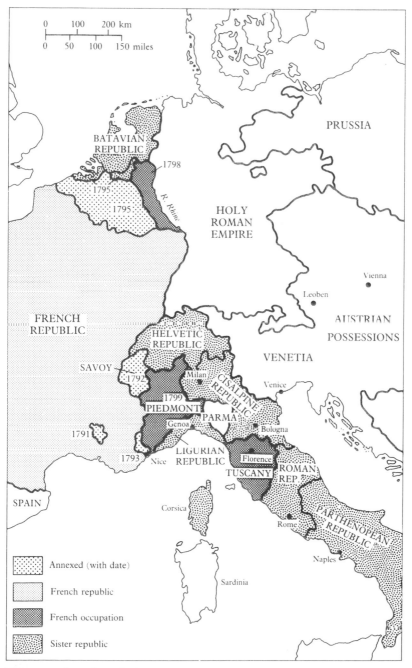

The expansion of revolutionary France

princes who had lost land there should be compensated by receiving ecclesiastical states elsewhere in Germany. Revolutionary France's power was at its height in the spring of 1798. It dominated west, central and southern Europe far more effectively than Louis XIV had ever done (see the map on page 111).

England was the only country at war with France by 1798. Napoleon was put in command of the Army of England to prepare for an invasion but he abandoned this idea when France failed to gain command of the sea. He decided instead to strike at England by invading Egypt. A French occupation of Egypt would interrupt British trade routes to India, would provide a base for a French expedition to India through the Red Sea and might persuade Indian princes to rise up against British rule. It would also enable France to control the eastern Mediterranean, and would provide both a market for French goods and a source of raw materials, especially cotton. In May 1798, Napoleon sailed from Toulon with 35 000 troops, captured Malta on the way and on 2 July arrived in Egypt. He captured Alexandria, defeated the Mamluks at the battle of the Pyramids and went on to take Cairo, all in the same month. It was another brilliant and rapid campaign but was negated on 1 August when Nelson captured or destroyed 11 out of 13 French ships of the line at Aboukir Bay. This left the French army cut off in Egypt.

*The defeat of France at the battle of the Nile (or Aboukir Bay) encouraged other countries to take up arms against her again. The Second Coalition was formed, and Russia, which had not taken part in previous fighting against France, declared war in December. Tsar Paul was incensed at the French seizure of Malta, of which he had declared himself protector in 1797. France declared war on Austria in March 1799 because she allowed Russian troops to move through her territory. Immediately war resumed, France occupied the rest of Italy; Piedmont was annexed to France, and Naples was turned into another 'sister' republic – the Parthenopean. These early successes were followed by a series of defeats. The French were pushed back to the Rhine by the Austrians, and the Russians advanced through northern Italy. The French withdrew from the whole of Italy, except Genoa, as the Russians moved into Switzerland. It appeared that France would be invaded for the first time in six years, but, as had happened before, France was saved by quarrels among the allies. Austria, instead of supporting Russia in Switzerland, sent her best troops north to the Rhine. This allowed the French to move on to the offensive in Switzerland, where the Russians were compelled to withdraw in the autumn of 1799. The danger to France was over.

e) The Jacobin Resurgence

The persecution of royalists since Fructidor had been severe, so they tended to keep away from the electoral assemblies in 1798. In the elections the Jacobins did well but had less than a third of the deputies. The Directory could be sure of a majority in the new legislature, yet the directors persuaded the Councils by the Law of 22 Floréal (11 May) to annul the election of 127 deputies, 86 of whom were suspected Jacobins. The deputies to replace those not allowed to sit were largely chosen by the directors, another contravention of the 1795 Constitution. The *coup d'état* of Floréal was less drastic than that of Fructidor but it had less justification: no-one could pretend that the Republic was in danger. Once again the Directory had shown its contempt for the wishes of the electors.

By 1798 there were only 270 000 men in the French army, so Jourdan proposed that conscription should be re-introduced, for the first time since 1793. The Councils approved this in September 1798. There was widespread resistance. Much of Belgium, where conscription was also applied, revolted in November and it took two months to put down the rising. Of the first draft of 203 000, only 74 000 reached the armies.

The 1799 elections once again showed the unpopularity of the Directory. Only 66 of 187 government candidates were elected. Among the rest there were about 50 Jacobins, including some who had been purged at Floréal. They were still a minority but many moderate deputies were now prepared to follow their lead. They had become disillusioned with the government, as news of military defeats reached Paris. The military situation was regarded as so desperate that the Councils were persuaded that emergency measures were needed and they passed laws proposed by Jacobins. In June 1799 Jourdan called for a new *levée en masse*: all men between 20 and 25 were to be called up immediately. As the armies were being pushed back into France the Republic could no longer pay for the war by foreign requisitions. A forced loan on the rich was therefore decreed, which was to raise 100 million livres and meant that the wealthy might have to give up as much as three-quarters of their income. The Law of Hostages of 12 July was even worse for the *notables*. Any areas resisting the new laws could be declared 'disturbed'. Local authorities could then arrest relatives of *émigrés*, nobles or rebels. They could be imprisoned, fined and their property confiscated to pay for the damage done by those causing disturbances. These measures seemed a return to the Terror of the Year II, when there had been arbitrary arrests and all the rich had been suspects, but still only 10 million livres of the forced loan had been collected by November. Conscription should have produced 402 000 troops but, as in 1798, there was widespread resistance and only 248 000 (60 per cent) joined the army. Many joined brigands or royalist rebels to avoid being called up. The Law of Hostages was hardly ever applied, because of opposition from local officials.

In 1799 there was a virtual collapse of government administration in the provinces. The Directory could not persuade local *notables* to accept office and had few troops to enforce its decrees. Local authorities were often taken over by royalists, who refused to levy forced loans, persecute non-juring priests or catch deserters. The National Guard was not large enough to keep order in the absence of regular troops, so substantial areas of the countryside were not policed at all. Brigandage was a result of the administrative collapse. By November 1799 there was civil war in the Ardèche: government commissioners were killed as quickly as they were replaced.

In the late summer of 1799 the military situation improved. The Russians were driven out of Switzerland in September. Sieyès, who had become a director, saw this as an opportunity to stage a *coup*. He wanted to strengthen the executive but knew that the Five Hundred would not agree to this and that it could not be done constitutionally. For a *coup* the support of the army was necessary. Who would be a reliable general? Moreau was approached but recommended Bonaparte, who had returned from Egypt on 10 October. 'There is your man', he told Sieyès. 'He will make your *coup d'état* far better than I can.'

f) Brumaire

On his way to Paris Bonaparte was greeted rapturously by the population, as the most successful of the republican generals and the one who had brought peace in 1797. He had made up his mind to play a leading role in French politics. He agreed to join Sieyès' *coup* but only on condition that a provisional government of three consuls should be set up, who would draft a new constitution.

Sieyès wanted to move the Councils to St Cloud, as in Paris the Jacobins in the Five Hundred were numerous enough to provide opposition to his plans. The Ancients, using as an excuse a terrorist plot, persuaded the Councils to move to St Cloud. Once there it became clear on 19 Brumaire (10 November) that the only plot was one organised by Sieyès. The Council of Five Hundred was furious, so Bonaparte reluctantly agreed to address both Councils. His appearance in the Five Hundred with armed grenadiers was greeted with cries of 'Outlaw' and 'Down with the tyrant'. He was physically attacked by Jacobin deputies and had to be rescued by fellow officers. It was not at all clear that the soldiers would take action against the elected representatives of the nation. Napoleon's brother Lucien, President of the Five Hundred, came to his rescue when he told the troops that some deputies were trying to assassinate their general. At this they took action and cleared the hall where the 500 were meeting. A rump of the Councils then approved a decree abolishing the Directory and replacing it with a provisional executive committee of three members, including Sieyès and Napoleon. The population, indifferent to the *coup*, accepted it apathetically. A poster in Paris showed how disillusioned many were with the Directory and what they hoped a change of regime would achieve:

1 France wants something great and long-lasting. Instability has been her downfall, and she now invokes steadiness. She has no desire for a monarchy . . . but she does want unity in the action of the power executing laws. She wants a free and independent
5 legislature . . . She wants her representatives to be peaceable conservatives, not unruly innovators. Finally, she wants to enjoy the benefits accruing from ten years of sacrifices.

Few realised the significance of the *coup d'état* of Brumaire. The Revolution was over.

g) Why did the Directory fail?

The directors had wanted to produce a stable government, which maintained the gains of the Revolution of 1789 whilst avoiding the extremes of Jacobin dictatorship or royalism. Their failure to obtain stability was partly due to the Constitution of the Year III, with its annual elections. It made no provision for settling disputes between the executive and legislative or for changing the Constitution in under nine years. The directors, therefore, interfered with the election results, to ensure they had a majority in the Councils. They purged the Councils in Fructidor 1797 and Floréal 1798. Napoleon told the Ancients that the Constitution had ceased to be observed: 'You yourselves destroyed it on 18 Fructidor, on 22 Floréal. . . . Nobody has any respect for it now.'

The Thermidorians had used the army to put down the risings of Prairial and Vendémiaire and the Directory had used it to carry out the *coup d'état* of Fructidor. Some historians, therefore, regard the Directory as dependent on the army and an army take-over as inevitable. Yet it was not the generals who planned the *coup* of Brumaire. Once again they were called in by the politicians, who assumed that they would then leave the scene to the civilians as they had done after Fructidor.

Most of the people who would normally have supported the Directory – owners of *biens*, the wealthy *notables* – were alienated by its policies, especially its forced loans. They showed this by refusing, in increasingly large numbers, to vote in the annual elections or to take up posts in local government. The population as a whole was apathetic. Public inertia may have helped the Directory to survive but it meant that there was no-one prepared to defend it. People were listless and lacking in enthusiasm because the war had gone on for so long and they wanted peace above all. Yet war had become a necessity for the Directory. It needed war to keep ambitious generals and unruly soldiers

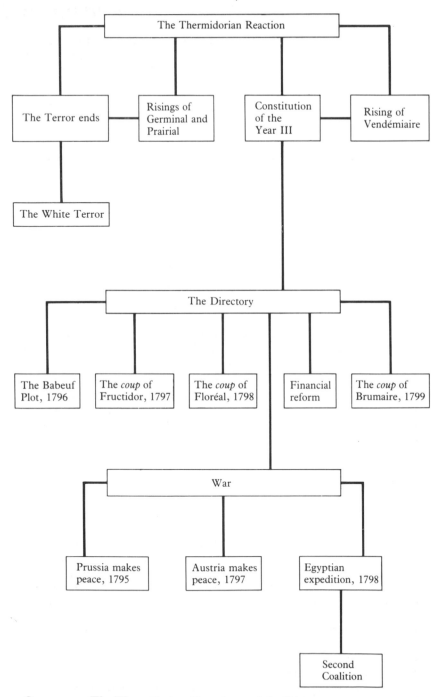

Summary – The Thermidorian Reaction and the Directory

out of France, to provide money for the French treasury and to produce the victories and the prestige which would enable the regime to survive. 'The Directory', wrote Napoleon in exile on St Helena, 'was overpowered by its own weakness: to exist it needed a state of war as other governments need a state of peace.' One of the reasons for Napoleon's popularity was that he had brought peace at Campo Formio in 1797. After this, war could have been avoided on the continent but for the actions of the Directory in extending French influence in Italy and Switzerland and in its approval of the Egyptian expedition. This led to the formation of the Second Coalition, military defeats, risings against France in the conquered territories and further royalist activity in France. Renewed war also produced a flurry of Jacobin activity, including a forced loan and the Law of Hostages. The Jacobins were never more than an urban minority and were no direct threat to the Directory but by reviving fears of a Terror like that of the Year II, they convinced many that the Directory could not, and should not, survive.

These events discredited the Directory and produced politicians who were not as attached to the republic as the *conventionnels* had been. Only 12 per cent of those elected to the Councils in 1799 had been members of the Convention and only five per cent were regicides. Over half the deputies chosen in 1799 were elected for the first time that year. These deputies were prepared to accept the view of Sieyès that the Constitution should be changed and that this involved getting rid of the Directory. They were not only prepared to welcome the new regime but took part in running it. Of 498 high officials of the Consulate 77 per cent had been deputies under the Directory. These men of the right and centre wanted stability and were prepared to accept an authoritarian regime to get it.

Making notes on 'The Thermidorian Reaction and the Directory'

Your notes on the period 1794–9 should help you to understand why the Terror came to an end, how the *sans-culottes* were finally crushed and why there was so much political instability. They should also make clear to you how the First Coalition was defeated and why a Second was formed. The following headings and sub-headings should help you:

1.   The Thermidorian Reaction
1.1. The Terror ends
1.2. The risings of Germinal and Prairial, 1795
1.3. The White Terror
1.4. The Constitution of the Year III. What were its weaknesses?
1.5. The rising of Vendémiaire, 1795

2.   The Directory
2.1. The Babeuf Plot, 1796
2.2. The *coup d'état* of Fructidor, 1797
2.3. Financial reform
2.4. War – Prussia and Austria make peace. Second Coalition formed
2.5. The Jacobin resurgence – the *coup* of Floréal, 1798
2.6. The *coup* of Brumaire, 1799
2.7. Why did the Directory fail?

Answering essay questions on 'The Thermidorian Reaction and the Directory'

You are very unlikely to find any questions specifically on the Thermidorian reaction and you will find few on the Directory. The most common question on the latter is 'Why did the Directory fail?' Make a list of all the reasons you can think of for the Directory's failure. When you have made your list, rearrange it to put the reasons in descending order of importance. Make sure you show the connections between them.

You are more likely to find questions which involve some of the information in this chapter but which also require knowledge of other chapters. Examples are:

1. 'What influence did the *sans-culottes* have on the French Revolution?'

You will find most of the answer to this question in Chapter 5 but your knowledge of the risings of Germinal and Prairial will form part of the answer.

2. 'What were the effects of foreign war on events inside France between 1792 and 1799?'

Much of the answer to this question will be found in Chapters 4 and 5 but there is a great deal in this chapter which should be considered. Make a list of events in the war. Which of these had repercussions inside France and why? What was the significance of these events?

Source-based questions on 'The Thermidorian Reaction and the Directory'

1   The Risings of 1795
Read carefully the report by Ruault on page 100 and that of a

government agent on page 105. Answer the following questions:
a) Why did farmers 'refuse to sell [their grain] for paper money'?
b) What was the situation 'at the end of April '93'?
c) In what ways had the government shown favour 'to enemies of democracy' and 'harshness . . . to former patriots'?
d) Which sections of the bourgeoisie had suffered and how?

2   The *coup* of Brumaire

Read carefully the words of the placard on page 115 and Napoleon's comments on the same page. Answer the following questions:
a) Is it true that 'instability has been her downfall'?
b) Why do you think the poster says 'She has no desire for a monarchy'?
c) What were the 'ten years of sacrifices'?
d) What does Napoleon mean by his references to '18 Fructidor, 22 Floréal'?

CHAPTER 7

The Impact of the Revolution

Contemporaries regarded the French Revolution as an event of major importance. The Duke of Dorset wrote to the English government as early as 16 July 1789 about 'the greatest Revolution that we know anything of'. Yet some historians, particularly English and American, have tended subsequently to play down its significance. They maintain that many of the reforms which took place during the Revolution – free trade, religious toleration, the end of venal offices and financial privileges – were all taking place under the *ancien régime*. They would have happened if there had been no Revolution. The rise of the bourgeoisie and the economic dominance of the British were also taking place before the Revolution and were not much affected by it. How true is this? In this chapter we shall be looking at what changes had taken place from 1789–99 which were lasting, who in France had gained and who had lost from the Revolution and what effect it had outside France.

1 The *Ancien Régime* Dismantled

Most of the *cahiers* in 1789 were moderate and none suggested the abolition of the monarchy. Yet within a short time, beginning with the August Decrees and Declaration of Rights, fundamental changes had taken place which swept away most of the institutions of the old regime. This has led historians, like the American G. V. Taylor, to maintain that it was not the revolutionaries who made the Revolution but the Revolution which made the revolutionaries. 'The revolutionary state of mind', he wrote, 'expressed in the Declaration of the Rights of Man and the decrees of 1789–91 was a product – and not a cause – of a crisis that began in 1787'.

The most famous of the abandoned institutions was that of the monarchy, abolished in 1792. This was not to be lasting, as the monarchy returned in 1814, although it was not to be the same as in 1789. Its powers were to be limited, particularly by an elected assembly which had the right to pass laws. Assemblies during the Revolution were hardly democratic as, after the primary assemblies, voting was confined to a small minority of property-holders. However, an elected legislature was to be one of the permanent changes brought about by the Revolution.

The reforms of the Constituent Assembly were to prove, as a whole, the most radical and the most lasting of the Revolution. The France of the *ancien régime* was dismembered and then reconstructed according to new principles. Most of the institutions of the old regime were abolished and were never to return. The legal distinction between Estates disappeared, as did the privileges of nobles, Church and *pays d'états* – although the nobility returned under Napoleon. The *généralités* and intendants, the old courts of law and the 13 *parlements* went too. The entire financial structure of the *ancien régime* was abandoned: direct taxes (the *taille, capitation* and *vingtième*); the Farmers-General; indirect taxes like the *gabelle* and *aides*; internal customs; venal offices, and the guilds and corporations all came to an end, along with other restrictive practices. The Church was drastically transformed by losing the tithe and its lands. The sale of the *biens nationaux* was the greatest change in land ownership in France for hundreds of years: a tenth of the land came on to the market at one time.

What replaced all that had been destroyed? The administrative structure of modern France was established: the departments, districts and communes; new regular courts of law for both criminal and civil cases; a centralised treasury; taxes from which no-one was exempt and the standardisation of weights and measures through decimalisation. Careers became open to talent in the bureaucracy, the army and the Church. All this – both the destructive and constructive work – was done in two years and was to be lasting. It was a remarkable achievement.

The three Estates of the *ancien régime* were also affected by the Revolution, though the extent to which they suffered or benefited is a matter for debate amongst historians.

2 The Social Impact

a) The Clergy

The Church was one of the losers in the Revolution. At an early stage it lost most of its wealth: its income from the tithe, its lands (which were taken over by the state) and its financial privileges, all of which were never recovered. Later its monopoly of education was removed, as was its control of poor relief and hospitals. The clergy became civil servants, as they were paid by the state and many were better off, as they received more money from the government than they had done before. Yet the Civil Constitution of the Clergy in 1790 produced a deep division within the Church. Those who did not accept it (about half the clergy) were persecuted as potential or actual counter-revolutionaries. Over 200 were killed in the September Massacres in 1792 and over 900 became official victims of the Terror. About 25 000 (a sixth of the clergy) emigrated or were deported. Many parishes were without a priest and during the dechristianisation campaign of the Year II most churches were closed. Even the constitutional clergy were abandoned, when the government refused to pay any clerical salaries in 1794. The state was separated from the Church and was to remain so until Napoleon's Concordat with the Pope in 1802. This rift had the unfortunate effect of embittering relations between Church and state for much of the nineteenth century. Church leaders looked on republicans as terrorists and persecutors and became suspicious of any attempt at reform. Republicans looked on the Church as obscurantist and as their main enemy, and wanted a return to the separation of Church and state. This would not be achieved until 1905.

b) The Nobility

Nobles were amongst the early leaders of the Revolution but withdrew from participation in public affairs from 1792 and were the greatest losers from the Revolution. They lost their feudal dues and this in some areas could amount to 60 per cent of their income. 'We never recovered', wrote the Marquis de la Tour du Pin, 'from the blow to our fortune delivered on that night' (4 August 1789). They also lost their financial privileges and consequently paid more in taxation. The *vingtième* and *capitation* usually took about five per cent of their income: the new land tax took 16 per cent. They lost their venal offices, their domination of high offices in the army, Church and state and even their right to bequeath their estates undivided to their oldest son (inheritances had to be divided equally amongst sons). In 1790 nobility itself was abolished. From the beginning of the Revolution some nobles emigrated, and eventually at least 16 500 went abroad (seven to eight per cent of all nobles). Their property was confiscated and this affected between a quarter and a half of all noble land. About 1200 nobles were executed during the Terror and many were imprisoned for months as suspects. Nobles, therefore, appear to have been the principal victims of the Revolution: many lost their lands and some their lives.

Recently historians have come to see this as an overdrawn picture. Nobles who stayed in France and were not persecuted during the Terror (the majority) retained their lands and never lost their position of economic dominance. Napoleon's tax-lists show that nobles were still amongst the wealthiest people in France. Of the 30 biggest taxpayers on the Lozère in 1811, 26 were nobles. Under Napoleon many *émigré* nobles returned to France and began to buy back their lands. In the Sarthe nobles had lost 100 000 acres but had recovered it all by 1830. Though precise statistics are not available for the whole of France, nobles overall may have recovered a quarter of the land they had lost. The ruling political élite in France both before and after the Revolution were large landowners and high officials, both noble and bourgeois, who came to be called *notables*. Owing to the economic disruption caused by the Revolution they continued to invest in land rather than industry, particularly when so much land came on to the market, cheaply, in the sale of *biens nationaux*. Francis d'Ivernois asked what Frenchman was mad enough

1 To risk his fortune in a business enterprise, or in competition
with foreign manufacturers? He would have to be satisfied with a
profit of ten, or at most twelve per cent, while the state offers him
the possibility of realising a return of thirty, forty or even fifty per
5 cent, if he places his money in one of the confiscated estates.

This group of *notables* governed France up to 1880 at least, and in this
sense the *ancien régime* continued well into the nineteenth century.

c) The Bourgeoisie

Marxists have always said that the French Revolution was a bourgeois
revolution. Historians like Albert Soboul maintain that the industrial
and commercial middle class carried through the Revolution.
'Businessmen and entrepreneurs', he writes, 'assumed the dominant
role hitherto occupied by inherited wealth ... soon these men, with
their willingness to take risks and their spirit of initiative, forsook
speculation and invested their capital in production, contributing in
this way to the rise of industrial capitalism.'

Nearly all English and American historians reject this view. They
point out that the bourgeoisie continued to invest in land rather than
industry, just as they had done before the Revolution. There were few
representatives of trade, finance or industry in the elected assemblies:
85 out of 648 deputies in the Constituent Assembly, 83 out of 891 in the
Convention. Small in numbers, they did not take the lead in political
affairs. There is no doubt that laws were passed which could eventually
benefit the industrialist – the abolition of internal customs barriers,
guilds and price controls, the prohibition of workers' associations and
the introduction of a uniform system of weights and measures. Yet it
was difficult to take advantage of these new laws until transport
improved sufficiently to create a national market and this had to wait
for the railways. Most merchants and manufacturers were worse off in
1799 than in 1789. The French Revolution was not, therefore, either in
its origins or development, carried out by the mercantile and industrial
bourgeoisie.

Yet the French Revolution *was* a bourgeois revolution, as the
bourgeoisie were its main beneficiaries and provided all its leaders after
1791. Many of the reforms of the Constituent Assembly were supposed
to apply to all citizens equally but only the bourgeoisie could take full
advantage of them. Workers and peasants benefited little when the
career became open to talent, as they were not educated. When the
biens were put up for sale they were sold in large lots and this too
benefited the middle classes, who owned between 30 and 40 per cent of
French land by 1799. The voting system also favoured the bourgeoisie,
as it was limited to property owners. Consequently, nearly all the
members of the various assemblies were bourgeois, who provided all

the ministers. Most of the revolutionary bourgeoisie were lawyers. There were 166 of them in the Constituent Assembly and another 278 were public officials, most of whom had a legal training. In the Convention they numbered 241 lawyers and 227 officials. These were the people who gained most from the Revolution, as they had the training to take advantage of the career open to talent. When venal offices were abolished, it appeared that this group would suffer, as their compensation was based on the values of their offices in 1770 and they were paid in *assignats*, which soon depreciated. However, many were elected to new local and national offices, which paid well. The central administration employed under 700 officials in the 1780s but by 1794, owing to the war, this number had risen to 6000. The number of officials in the country as a whole increased five-fold to about 250 000, about ten per cent of the bourgeoisie. Bourgeois had always filled the lower and middle ranks of the judiciary and the administration. With the Revolution they took over the highest posts too, which had all been held by nobles. Their dominance of the administration was to continue throughout the nineteenth century.

There were bourgeois who did not benefit from the Revolution: merchants of the Atlantic ports and manufacturers of luxury goods and *rentiers*, who were paid in *assignats*, which lost most of their value. In 1797 *rentiers* lost most of their investments in Ramel's 'bankruptcy of the two-thirds'. Nevertheless, most bourgeois did well out of the Revolution and would accept only those regimes which promised to maintain their gains.

d) The Peasantry

It is almost impossible to divide peasants into separate categories: landowners, tenant farmers, sharecroppers and labourers. Though there were some of each in the villages, most peasants did not fall into any single group. The majority held some of their land freehold, rented other parts and from time to time sold their labour.

The peasantry registered a mixture of gains and losses during the Revolution. Many lost their income from domestic industry, when there was a depression in textiles. Others saw their rents rise by as much as a quarter, when landlords were allowed to add the value of the abolished tithe to their rents. Conscription, in 1793 and again in 1798, affected all and, with dechristianisation in 1793–4, turned many peasants against the Revolution. Those who produced for the market were badly affected by the Maximum on the price of grain in the Year II and by the requisitions to feed the towns and the army. The result of all these measures was a widespread, popular resistance movement, which in the Vendée flared into open revolt. In Brittany and Normandy, where the abolition of feudalism produced few benefits as most peasants rented their land, there was *chouannerie*. In the south too there was widespread opposition, as the Revolution seemed to benefit the rich Protestants of towns like Nîmes rather than the local Catholics. In some areas this opposition was caught up in royalist counter-revolution but peasants generally did not wish to see a return to the *ancien régime*, which might bring with it a restoration of feudal dues. Their opposition was therefore anti-revolutionary rather than counter-revolutionary. They wanted stability, their old way of life and the exclusion of 'foreigners' (officials from Paris or from outside their own district) from their affairs. Resistance produced repression and executions – nearly 60 per cent of the official victims of the Terror were peasants or workers and many more were killed when the army devastated the Vendée.

Yet most peasants benefited in one way or another from the Revolution. All gained from the abolition of indirect taxes and their total tax burden was reduced. Those who owned land benefited from the abolition of feudal dues and the tithe. In the north and east, where the Church owned much land, peasants were able to buy some of the *biens*, though it was usually the richer peasants who were able to do this. In the south-west even share-croppers bought *biens* and became supporters of the Revolution. Peasants also gained from inflation, which grew steadily worse between 1792–7. They were able to pay off their debts with depreciating *assignats* and tenants were able to redeem their leases. Judicial and local government reforms were to the advantage of all peasants. The abolition of seigneurial justice was a great boon, as it was replaced by a much fairer system. The justice of the peace in each *canton* provided cheap and impartial justice. The right of self-government granted to local authorities favoured the peasants too, especially at the municipal level, where councils were elected and filled by peasants. Over a million people took part in these councils in 1790 and many more later. In the north and east most of these were rich peasants, though in Poitou poorer peasants, tenant farmers and share-croppers took control. Peasants looked on municipal self-government as one of their greatest gains from the Revolution. Both the self-governing commune and justices of the peace survived to play important roles in the nineteenth century.

The poor peasants, the landless day-labourers, are usually regarded as sufferers from the Revolution. They did not benefit from the abolition of feudal dues and they were hit hard by the inflation from 1792–7, as wages failed to rise as quickly as prices. Many relied on cottage industry for survival and when the market for this collapsed, they became destitute. However, all was not loss. They did gain from the abolition of indirect taxes. From 1797–9 they gained from deflation, so that by 1799 their real wages were higher than they had been in 1789.

The Revolution, therefore, affected the peasants in different ways but for most (as for most bourgeois) their gains outweighed their losses, especially for those who owned land. Lecointe-Puyraveau, a government commissioner in the Deux-Sèvres, summed up the impact of the

Revolution on the peasant. He wrote in 1798 that the peasant

1 might well have complained [about conscription and requisition-
ing] but he has sold his remaining foodstuffs at extraordinary
prices and for three years has been able to settle his lease with the
modest production of the farmyard . . . As for the more intelligent
5 kind of cultivator knowing how to read and write, he has been
called to municipal office. This has flattered him and the satisfaction derived from issuing orders has given him a taste for the new
regime and he has attached himself to it.

e) Urban Workers and the Poor

The *sans-culottes* had welcomed the Revolution and had done a great
deal to ensure that it was successful, in storming the Bastille and in
bringing the royal family to Paris in the October Days of 1789. They
were to be bitterly disappointed by the first fruits of the Revolution.
Many became unemployed as the *parlements* were closed and nobles
emigrated. Guilds were abolished in 1791, which was of benefit to
apprentices but not their masters. Those still in work were forbidden to
strike. They played a leading role again in 1792, when they toppled the
monarchy, and in 1793, when the Committee of Public Safety had to
give way to many of their demands, such as a maximum price on bread.
However, the bourgeois revolutionary leaders were not prepared in the
long run to grant most of what they wanted. The urban workers
disliked a free, market economy yet this was imposed on them in 1794,
with the result that prices rose dramatically. The bad harvest and harsh
winter of 1794–5 reduced them to despair and the risings of Germinal
and Prairial, which were crushed. After that workers played no political
role in the Revolution. Their economic fortunes continued to decline in
1797, owing to the inflation caused by the fall of the *assignats*. Wages
rose but much more slowly than prices. There was, however, a revival
in the last years of the Directory from 1797–9, when deflation ensured
that real wages were higher than they had been for a very long time.
These were also years of good harvests, when the price of bread
dropped to two sous a pound (it was 14 sous in July 1789).

The poor suffered more than most during the Revolution. In normal
times about a quarter of the population of big cities relied on poor
relief. This number increased with the rise in unemployment, yet at the
same time their means of obtaining relief were disappearing. The main
source of help for the poor had been the Church, which had paid for
this out of income from the tithe. When the tithe was abolished and
church lands nationalised, the Church could no longer pay for aid to the
poor. If the poor were ill they had been cared for in hospitals also
provided by the Church and these were affected in the same way by the

Church's loss of income. They closed. The Constitution of 1793 said that all citizens had a right to public support but revolutionary governments were always short of money and nothing was done. As late as 1847 the number of hospitals in France was 42 per cent less than in 1789, though the population was seven million more. The result of the decline in the Church's role in providing poor relief and hospitals was that the poor were unable to cope with the economic crisis of 1794–5, when a bad harvest was followed by a harsh winter. Many died, either from starvation or from diseases, which the undernourished could not fight off. In Rouen the mortality rate doubled in 1795–6 and trebled the year after. There was also a marked rise in the number of suicides. The poor responded in the only ways they knew: they joined bands of brigands, which were endemic in many parts of France in the last years of the Directory.

3 The Economy

Marxists believe that by getting rid of feudalism, ending the monopolies of the guilds and unifying the national market, the Revolution, in Soboul's words, 'marked a decisive stage in the transition from feudalism to capitalism'. Most English historians treat such an interpretation with disdain. They maintain that the Revolution retarded, rather than promoted, the development of capitalism in France and that it was an economic disaster. The most rapidly expanding sector of the French economy up to 1791 was overseas trade. In that year a slave revolt broke out on the West Indian island of San Domingo, which provided three-quarters of France's colonial trade. This was followed in 1793 by war with Britain, when the French coast was blockaded. Prosperous Atlantic seaports like Bordeaux and Nantes suffered severely, as did the industries in the hinterland – sugar refineries, linen and tobacco manufacture – which had depended on them. In 1797 France had only 200 ocean-going vessels, a tenth of the number of 1789. French exports fell by 50 per cent in the 1790s. Foreign trade had accounted for 25 per cent of France's gross domestic product in 1789: by 1796 it was down to nine per cent.

War had a varied effect on French industries. Some benefited, as there was a demand for cloth for uniforms and iron and coal for the production of arms. The cotton industry gained most of all. It had been virtually ruined by English competition but with the war and French conquests it revived. English goods were kept out of territories under French control, so that French cotton production increased four-fold between the 1780s and 1810. This, however, was a short-term gain and could not be sustained. Once the war was over in 1815 cotton was hit again by British competition and some of the largest French manufacturers went bankrupt. During the war there was a shift in the location of industries from the Atlantic to the Rhine. This favoured cities such as Strasbourg, which grew rich on the continental transit trade. But other areas and industries did not do so well. Supplies of raw materials were disrupted by the war and foreign markets were lost. The linen industry in Brittany (which had exported to the West Indies and South America) fell by a third, industrial production at Marseille by three-quarters. By 1799 production had fallen overall to two-thirds of its pre-war level. A further misfortune suffered by industry was the inflation of 1792–7, which meant that there was little investment. When paper money was withdrawn in 1797 industry faced other problems. There was a shortage of cash, interest rates were high and agricultural prices (and therefore the peasant market for industrial goods) collapsed.

Agriculture stagnated during the Revolution. Production kept pace with population growth but this was done by bringing more land into cultivation rather than by improving productivity, which did not rise until the 1840s. Yields remained low and old-fashioned techniques continued. Oxen were still used for pulling wooden (not metal) ploughs and the harvest was cut with sickles rather than scythes. Most peasants produced for subsistence only and plots remained small, especially when, by law, a peasant's land was divided up equally amongst his sons.

The Revolution, then, held up the development of the French economy, which grew only slowly down to the 1840s. Although France had fallen behind Britain industrially by 1789, the gap between them increased even more markedly during the Revolution. It was not until the coming of the railways that French industrialists could take advantage of a national market. Railways lowered the cost of transport and gave a great boost to the heavy industries of coal, iron, and steel. Only then did factory production become the norm. This happened between 1830 and 1870 and brought to an end the economic *ancien régime*, something the Revolution had failed to do.

4   The Impact on Europe

One effect of the French Revolution was that it changed the map of Europe. France lost nearly all the territories she annexed, except Avignon, though she was to recover Savoy and Nice in 1860. Elsewhere changes were made which were lasting. The city states of Genoa and Venice never recovered an independent existence and Austria's loss of Belgium was permanent. The Holy Roman Empire was drawing to an end and the process of redrawing the map of Germany had begun by getting rid of the ecclesiastical states. Outside Europe, the revolutionary wars had led to Britain seizing Ceylon and the Cape of Good Hope, territories she was to retain into the twentieth century.

The French Revolution also affected the ideas people held and therefore the policies they pursued. When so many established institutions, beliefs and practices were attacked – monarchies, religion, privilege – some writers came to their defence and the ideology of conservatism was born. Edmund Burke defended tradition, religious faith, and slow change. He argued that violent revolutions produced chaos and should be avoided, adding:

1 It were better to forget, once for all, the *encyclopédie* . . . and to revert to the old rules and principles which have hitherto made princes great and nations happy.

Burke influenced the work of statesmen like Metternich after 1815. Rulers, who had supported reform in the 1780s, now regarded it as dangerous and so there was a conservative reaction which lasted well into the nineteenth century.

Conservative ideas were not the only ones produced by, or in reaction to, the French Revolution. Wherever French armies went there was a great diffusion of French ideas and methods, as they created republics, established representative government, seized church lands and abolished privilege. These reforms could be, and often were, reversed when the French withdrew. But ideas could not be eradicated so easily. Concepts such as the sovereignty of the people, equality before the law, freedom from arbitrary arrest, freedom of speech and association and the career open to talent all had a wide appeal. Many of these ideas were ignored in practice during the Revolution but they nevertheless contributed to the revolutionary myth, which influenced so many outside France, particularly middle-class liberals. Liberalism in the nineteenth century owed much to the French Revolution.

Nationalism was another powerful force which the French Revolution produced. Revolutionary leaders had deliberately set out to create a unified nation, by getting rid of all provincial privileges, internal customs dues and different systems of law. Sovereignty, said the Declaration of Rights, resides in the nation. Symbols like the *tricolore* (the new national flag), the *Marseillaise* (adopted as the national anthem in 1795), huge national festivals, (the first of which was the *Fête de la Fédération* on 14 July 1790 to celebrate the fall of the Bastille), were all used to rouse patriotic fervour. Army life also helped to create loyalty to the nation. It was often the first time peasants had been outside their own locality or come into contact with the French language. However, the success of revolutionary leaders in uniting the nation should not be exaggerated. As late as the Third Republic peasants in the south and west still had local rather than national loyalties and looked on people from outside their area as unwelcome 'foreigners'. Yet France's success in her wars was often attributed to nationalism and the *élan* of the French soldier. Many outside of France were inspired by the right to self-determination which the French proclaimed. In Italy national feeling was aroused for the first time, partly by the French example, and in Germany people also began to look to the formation of a united Germany.

A great legacy of the French Revolution was the right to resist oppression, which was enshrined in the Constitution of 1793. Kolokotrones, a Greek bandit and patriot, said that according to his judgement

1 the French Revolution and the doings of Napoleon opened the eyes of the world. The nations knew nothing before and the people thought that kings were gods upon the earth and that they were bound to say that whatever they did was well done. Through
5 this present change it is more difficult to rule the people.

The first half of the nineteenth century became the 'Age of Revolutions' largely because the French provided a model, which others sought to copy, leading Thomas Paine to comment:

1 From what we now see, nothing of reform in the political world ought to be held improbable. It is an age of Revolutions, in which everything may be looked for.

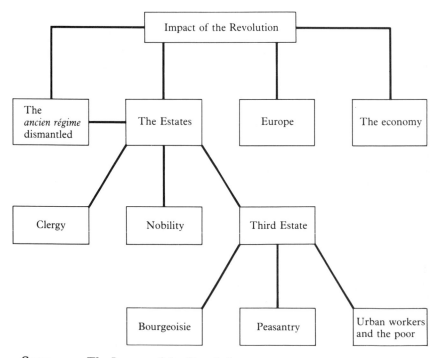

Summary – The Impact of the Revolution

Making notes on 'The Impact of the Revolution'

Your notes should help you to understand what lasting changes the French Revolution brought about, both inside and outside France. The following headings and sub-headings should help you:

1.   The *Ancien Régime* Dismantled
2.   The Social Impact
2.1. The clergy
2.2. The nobility
2.3. The bourgeoisie
2.4. The peasantry
2.5. Urban workers and the poor
3.   The Economy
4.   The Impact on Europe

Answering essay questions on 'The Impact of the Revolution'

You will have to refer to your notes from other chapters when you answer questions on the Revolution as a whole. This chapter should help you to draw some of the threads together. Typical questions are:

1. 'Which changes in France in the period 1789–99 were enduring?'

Many of the enduring changes took place from 1789–91 under the Constituent Assembly. So you will have to look very carefully at your notes on Chapters 3 and 4. Make a list of the changes under such headings as: social groups, institutions, the economy, territory. Then divide them up into two sections: reforms which were lasting and those which were not. Try to decide whether some of the lasting changes were more important than others and why.

2. 'How changed was the France of 1799 from that of 1789?'

To answer the second part of this question you will have to refer to your notes on Chapter 2. Make a list of the main features of the *ancien régime*. In a separate column note whether these features remained in 1799 and why.

Glossary

aides – duties on food and drink.

anobli – a recently ennobled commoner.

armées revolutionnaires – civilian armies in 1793–4, formed to requisition grain from the countryside to feed the cities.

assignat – paper money in general use from 1791–7.

banalités – the right of a *seigneur* to compel his tenants to use his mill, bakery and winepress.

biens nationaux – property of the Church and *émigrés* seized by the state and sold at auction.

bourgeoisie – urban middle classes (e.g. merchants, bankers, lawyers).

cahiers – lists of grievances drawn up by the three Estates before the Estates-General met.

capitation – poll tax, paid by all except the clergy.

champart – harvest dues paid by peasants to their *seigneurs*.

Chouans – peasants in Brittany and Normandy who fought against the Revolution from 1793–6.

Commune – the municipal government of Paris.

conventionnel – a member of the Convention.

corvée – the peasants' obligation to do unpaid labour on the roads.

don gratuit – 'free gift' given by the Church to the King instead of paying taxes.

émigrés – people who had fled from France during the Revolution.

fédérés – National Guardsmen who came from the provinces to Paris in 1792 and helped to overthrow the monarchy.

Feuillants – moderate constitutional monarchists who left the Jacobin Club in July 1791.

gabelle – a tax on salt.

généralités – financial areas of the *ancien régime*.

jeunesse dorée – 'gilded youth'. Middle class youth who took part in the White Terror and attacked Jacobins and *sans-culottes*.

journée – day when the *sans-culottes* took to the streets, often to intimidate the elected Assembly.

laboureur – *not* a labourer but a well-off peasant, who grew enough food for his own needs.

lettres de cachet – sealed letters, issued by the King, by which people could be imprisoned without trial.

levée en masse – mobilisation of the whole French nation for war in August 1793.

lit de justice – ceremony at which the King insisted on the *parlements* registering royal edicts.

livre – main unit of money, the equivalent of 20 *sous*.

lods et ventes – feudal due paid to the *seigneur* when property was sold.

maximum – price fixed for grain and basic necessities.

menu peuple – the common people.

Montagnards – Name given to Jacobin deputies as they sat on the top seats (The Mountain) in the Assembly.

noblesse de robe – magistrates who had bought offices which conferred nobility.

octrois – duties on goods entering towns.

parlements – 13 high courts of appeal which had the right to register royal edicts and criticise them (*not* to be confused with 'parliaments').

parlementaire – a member of a *parlement*.

pays d'états – provinces near French frontiers which had special rights and privileges.

rente – a fixed income from investments (e.g. government stock).

rentier – a person living on *rentes*.

sans-culottes – urban workers: wage-earners and small property owners.

Sections – the 48 units of local self-government in Paris.

seigneur – lord of the manor.

taille – the main direct tax before the Revolution, paid by all commoners.

tricolore – the red, white and blue national flag.

vingtième – tax on income, supposedly of five per cent but often more, paid by all except clergy.

Further Reading

There are two outstanding books on the French Revolution as a whole:

William Doyle, *The Oxford History of the French Revolution* (OUP 1989) and
D. M. G. Sutherland, *France 1789–1815: Revolution and Counter-revolution* (Fontana 1985).

As the sub-title implies, this second book treats the opposition to the Revolution much more fully than is usual in general histories of the Revolution.

There has been an enormous amount of research on the French Revolution in the last 20 years, so books written before that need to be treated with great care. For example:

Alfred Cobban, *A History of Modern France, Vol. 1, 1715–99* (Penguin 1957).

This book is out of date, particularly on the origins of the Revolution.
One volume histories which are still useful if somewhat dated, are:

F. Furet and D. Richet, *The French Revolution* (Weidenfeld 1970),
A. Goodwin, *The French Revolution* (Hutchinson, 5th edition 1970),
Norman Hampson, *A Social History of the French Revolution* (Routledge 1966),
George Rudé, *Revolutionary Europe, 1783–1815* (Fontana 1964),
Albert Soboul, *A Short History of the French Revolution, 1789–1799* (University of California Press 1965) and
M. J. Sydenham, *The French Revolution* (Batsford 1965).

There are numerous books on different aspects of the Revolution. On the *ancien régime* see:

C. B. Behrens, *The Ancien Régime* (Thames and Hudson 1967), and
Peter Robert Campbell, *The Ancien Régime in France* (Blackwell, Historical Association Studies 1988).

The classic account of the origins of the Revolution is:

Georges Lefebvre, *The Coming of the French Revolution* (Princeton 1947).

This book is arguably his best book and is certainly the easiest to read.

An excellent summary of recent research is:

William Doyle, *The Origins of the French Revolution* (OUP revised edition 1989).

The only book, and a very good one, on why France went to war is:

T. C. W. Blanning, *The Origins of the French Revolutionary Wars* (Longman 1986).

For the *sans-culottes* see:

Gwyn A. Williams, *Artisans and Sans-culottes* (Libris, reprinted 1989).

and for the peasantry:

P. M. Jones, *The Peasantry in the French Revolution* (CUP 1988).

This is a superb book, much fuller in its coverage than its title indicates.

The Terror is discussed, succinctly and incisively, in:

Norman Hampson, *The Terror in the French Revolution* (Historical Association pamphlet, General Series 103).

There are two comparatively recent biographies of Robespierre:

George Rudé, *Robespierre* (Collins 1975) and
Norman Hampson, *The Life and Opinions of Maximilien Robespierre* (Duckworth 1974).

This second volume is a difficult book but it is worth persevering with.

The best book on the Directory is:

Martin Lyons, *France Under the Directory* (CUP 1975).

There are many chapters which are of little use to A-level candidates but used selectively it will be invaluable. Also of benefit is:

M. J. Sydenham, *The First French Republic, 1792–1804* (Batsford 1974).

Two books, both short and very stimulating, discuss interpretations of the Revolution:

T. C. W. Blanning, *The French Revolution – Aristocrats v Bourgeois?* (Macmillan Education 1987) and
Alfred Cobban, *The Social Interpretation of the French Revolution* (CUP 1964).

Sources on France in Revolution

There are two excellent collections of documents:

John Hardman, *The French Revolution, 1785–1795* (Arnold 1981) and
R. Cobb and C. Jones, *The French Revolution, 1789–1795* (Simon and Schuster 1989).

This book also contains short and valuable articles on various aspects of the Revolution and some splendid illustrations.
Shorter collections of documents are in:

L. W. Cowie, *The French Revolution* (Macmillan Education 1987) and
D. G. Wright, *Revolution and Terror in France, 1789–1795* (Longman 1974).

Acknowledgements

The publishers would like to thank The Bridgeman Art Library for permission to reproduce the illustration on page 31.

Index